When Dublin was the Capital
Northern Life Remembered

Allison Murphy

Belcouver Press
2000

Belcouver Press
Box 117, 1857 West 4th Avenue
Vancouver, B.C. V6J 1M4
Canada

Belcouver Press
44 Shore Road
Portaferry, Co. Down
Northern Ireland BT22 1JZ
United Kingdom

Canadian Cataloguing in Publication Data: A CIP catalogue record for this book is available from the National Library, Ottawa.

Includes bibliographical references.
ISBN 0 - 9699464 -3 - 0
1. Ireland - Civilisation - 20th Century. I. Title

Printed by Spectrum Press
East Belfast Industrial Park
308 Albertbridge Road
Belfast BT5 4GX

Contents

Illustrations

Acknowledgements

I wish to thank my informants Norman Douglas, Ena McKenna, Teresa Marlow, Johnny Marquis, John Parkinson, Annie Stewart and Mary Thompson for sharing their memories and their time with me and for providing me with family photographs. I am indebted to Linda Wilkinson for all her support and to Helene Turner for taking the time to send me the photograph that helps to illustrate the book's cover. I would also like to thank Ruby Purdy and Robert Morrow for their photographs, and Gerry Dawe, Jack Foster and Aodan MacPoilin for their encouragement. My husband Rowland Murphy exercised to my great advantage his usual efficiency in solving innumerable practical problems in logistics and transport. For permission to inspect their relevant archives, I wish to thank the staff of the Belfast Telegraph and the Ulster Folk & Transport Museum.

Illustrations on pp. 1, 11, 12, 23, 26, 30, 33, 36, 43, 46, 51, 76, 80, 87, 88, 107, 110, 115, 121, 142, 148 by kind permission of the Trustees of the National Museums and Galleries of Northern Ireland; illustrations on pp. 14, 18, 35, 55, 56, 139 courtesy of the National Library of Ireland.

This book has received support from the Cultural Diversity Programme of the Community Relations Council, which aims to encourage acceptance and understanding of cultural diversity. The views expressed do not necessarily reflect those of the Northern Ireland Community Relations Council. The publisher wishes here to thank this body that made publication of this book possible.

This book is dedicated in hope for the future to my own little grandson, Ben.

ALLISON MURPHY

INTRODUCTION

Group of men at Belfast Dog Show, 1909.
(Hogg Collection, Ulster Museum)

None but an Ulsterman can fairly criticise Ulstermen. In theory we hated one another bitterly, but practice did not follow at theory's heels.

Lynn Doyle *An Ulster Childhood* (1921)

'Most history has been written 'from above', from the perspective of the powerful privileged few. In rewriting history "from below" oral history can create a more accurate and authentic picture of the past.'
(Stephen Humphries, *Handbook of Oral History*, 1984)

The idea for this book arose out of conversations with an elderly relative whose memories of Belfast [Ireland] in the decade before partition, i.e. 1910 to 1920, seemed strangely out of line with many historical interpretations of the period which I held and had read. It seemed to me that most of what I had read, and subsequently believed, was based on the major events of history, and that was in most cases history 'from above'. I felt, therefore, that an historically minded examination of the period 1910-1920 would perhaps shed some insights into why what had been written by historians differed so much from what was remembered by someone who was alive at the time.

For this reason I decided that a fair approach would be to examine what had been written historically about the period in order to confirm my impressions. The next step would be to examine source materials, such as newspapers and school textbooks, to discover what had actually been written at and about the time and would have been read by the people then alive. Finally I would compare these findings with what someone who was alive then remembered happening in the day to day activities of what constitutes ordinary life.

Since I was born in Belfast and have lived there for most of my life, I realised that to record the memories of only one person would provide a one-sided view which would be either Protestant- or Catholic-orientated and could be considered as unrepresentative or biased. Among other differences, such as class, the issue of religion was a salient one. As I had an elderly relative who is a Protestant male it was necessary to find other people who were of a different sex and/or religion and had an equally good recall of the period. The oral historian Paul Thompson asserts that oral evidence makes for a history which is not just richer, more vivid and heart-rending, but truer, and that accurate memory is much more likely when it meets a social interest and need. I decided, therefore, to concentrate the research on activities which would have been of most interest to young people at the time. They would have been at school during most of the period and would have engaged in leisure pursuits after school and at weekends. Their attitudes to those of the 'other' religion would have been learned in their homes, and a knowledge of places they went and those they played with might indicate what those attitudes were. They would have gone shopping, on excursions or on holidays, to churches, to sporting events or to places of entertainment.

In particular, this informal study would consider whether young people who lived in the north of Ireland between 1910 and 1920 would have acted as though they lived in a society which was divided along religious lines, or would have considered themselves as living in such a society. According to the social anthropologist, Rosemary Harris, a real understanding of any socially divided society depends on an examination of society at the grass roots level as well as on the analysis of the political and economic structure. She felt that the separation between the Catholic and Protestant spheres in Northern Ireland, at the time of which she was writing, the 1950s, was manifested in marriage, education and organisational membership but that there was a considerable area within which Catholics and Protestants shared a common culture. My study will examine some aspects of society at the 'grass roots level' before 1920 to see whether a 'common culture' was shared at that time.

My focus on these elements of popular culture is undoubtedly informed by my own knowledge and experience of living in a divided, sectarian society, though I was fortunate to spend all my teenage years in the sixties, pre-troubles Belfast. I grew up in the era of Terence O'Neill and Sean Lemass when many young people believed that a new Northern Ireland was on the horizon. We Catholics and Protestants danced together to Van Morrison and Them in the Rhythm & Blues Club on Friday nights, spent lunchtimes on the Plaza dance floor and passed afternoons in discussion and flirtation in Isobeal's coffee bar. We thought that mixed religion romances were normal and scoffed at our parents for daring to ask the religion of our boyfriends.

We were the new educated generation who had benefited from the 1947 Education Act and had attained the heady heights of grammar school. We would ensure that the future of Northern Ireland would be free from injustice and we sang 'Kevin Barry' and 'The Sash' to each other's tune to show our lack of bigotry. Those of us who were of unionist stock knew that there had been many years of misrule and wanted to atone for the sins of our fathers. Those of us of nationalist stock wanted our fair share of justice and employment, the Beatles and Bob Dylan. We all passionately supported the Civil Rights movement but never the violence that ensued. That drove a wedge between Protestants and Catholics that sent many scuttling back to their respective sectarian corners, as well as to universities south of the border and across the water.

Sectarianism has now come to mean, especially in Ireland, an excessive and fanatical adherence to the tenets of one's own sect to the point of discrimination against those not of the sect and is wholly derogatory. It is used as a synonym for, variously, bias, bigotry, intolerance, prejudice, discrimination, as well as negative stereotyping and false consciousness. Sectarianism extends beyond jobs and housing in Northern Ireland and has led to a divided community in terms of services, education and leisure pursuits. It is assumed to have had continuous meaning and to have been confrontational both before and after the partition of Ireland in 1920.

In his book *The Widening Gulf* the historian Dennis Kennedy states that after partition the attitude of most Protestants hardened towards their Catholic neighbours, but he does not give any description of what those attitudes had been before partition, or reveal on what he bases this statement. If oral history can create a more accurate and authentic picture of the past, then it seems logical to examine more than history books in order to establish what exactly Protestant and Catholic attitudes to each other were in the decade before partition. Since culture is formed in the home, church, school, playground and workplace, it would surely be useful to examine contemporary materials and to record the memories and opinions of those who were alive at the time.

In order to understand any change in attitudes that may have taken place, some aspects of popular culture of the period must be scrutinised for clues as to how divided a society it actually was in the decade immediately preceding partition. Newspapers of the period can provide details of contemporary events and give an indication of how people were spending their leisure time. Photographs may provide further illumination, as can contemporary literature, as well as histories of organisations then operating. An examination of school curricula provides evidence of what was being taught to those educated in the decade (though not necessarily what they were learning). Since written evidence is selected, shaped and filtered then oral history can be used to supplement this evidence, providing confirmation, filling in gaps and supplying an account of how ordinary people acted and interacted during the period. This evidence will be examined to see to what extent education and leisure activities were divided along sectarian lines in the north of Ireland from 1910 to 1920.

For a definition of sectarianism, I agree with Anthony Buckley that in Ireland sectarianism is really that sense of peoplehood, more generally called ethnicity, found throughout the world. My upbringing in Belfast leads me to believe, like Buckley, that the religious and political tags which are given to people in Ireland have only a subsidiary place and of much greater importance is the practical way people interact with each other. I want to see whether or not one can find sources which will illuminate further how people interacted with each other before partition and explore the ways in which different sources of information elicit different and sometimes contradictory findings.

A study of education and entertainment should provide a large amount of data which will give a greater insight into lifestyles and activities of the period. These data will be placed in the context of the major world, national and local events which were occurring at that time. Oral history may then be used to supplement this evidence, filling in gaps and considering the process from the point of view of those who were directly involved. It will also represent the feelings of the people accurately for, as the American folklorist J.B. Toelken states, history as seen through the lives of great personages gives us only a partial view of the real course of time. He points out that too often history deals only with the grand events of the past and neglects the fact that history has more farmers than generals. That the past contains just as many women as men has also been long neglected and a history which deals with only major events and people, usually male, cannot give us a complete picture.

Any examination of material written about the north-east of Ireland shows that the society therein is often paradoxical. Rosemary Harris wrote of 'prejudice and tolerance'; another anthropologist, Elliot Leyton, has written of 'opposition and integration'; and the historian F.S.L.Lyons spoke of 'unity and diversity'. Even these can oversimplify. As R.F.Foster, the historian, has stated: 'we should be seeking out the interactions, paradoxes and subcultures, if only to rearrange the pieces in more surprising patterns'.

This book will attempt to appraise whether people who lived in the north of Ireland in the decade before partition had access to, and engaged in, a common way of life or were divided by class or sectarian issues. A from-below history of the decade before partition might show that varieties of Irishness can be complementary rather than competing.

CHAPTER ONE
SETTING THE SCENE

In the eighteenth century the greatest industrial growth in Ireland took place in Ulster. An important merchant culture developed and it was a time of commercial expansion, especially in the area around the provincial capital, Belfast. Domestic spinning became widespread, huge flour mills were built, the textile and provisioning trades grew and Belfast soon had a Chamber of Commerce, a harbour Corporation and a White Linen Hall. Although there were great regional variations in prosperity, and many of the poor were really poor, there was a powerful, wealthy middle class who carried on the bulk of trade.

By the late eighteenth century, therefore, the seeds of the growth of industrialisation in the north-east of Ireland had been planted with the establishment of foundries, ropeworks, sugar refining, vitriol factories and linen manufacturing. As the century ended, there was an increase in imports and exports because of the demand in England as a result of the growth of towns during the Industrial Revolution. The Act of Union in 1801 harmonised this trade and provided a reasonably stable environment in which industrialisation could prosper. Belfast was a thriving, trading city whose population had grown from 8,500 in 1757 to 20,000 as the nineteenth century began.

The boom in cotton appears to have pushed Belfast into the factory age and made it accountable for a quarter of total Irish imports of cotton wool and yarn at the beginning of the century. This figure was to double in the following twenty years and the boom, sustained by the buoyant Napoleonic war economy, lasted until the end of protection in 1825. At this time mechanical spinning was invented and when Thomas Mulholland's cotton mill was burnt out in 1828, he decided, either brilliantly or luckily, to rebuild his mill for flax spinning. A mechanised linen industry rapidly began to flourish, although weaving was still a handloom, cottage industry. Other mill-owners followed Mulholland's example and by the 1860s, when steam power was applied to the weaving of linen, there were thirty-two flax spinning mills in Belfast and the surrounding area and linen exports were higher than ever before.

Such exports required a large port and for the first quarter of the century the harbour in Belfast, which had been little better than an anchorage, had been continuously deepened by using the sand for ballast for outgoing vessels. By 1835 it had already become the first port in Ireland in value of trade. As this trade continued to expand, the Harbour Commissioners (formerly the Ballast Board), who appear to have been very far-seeing, planned to dredge the Lough and thereby create three artificial islands, the largest of which, the Queen's Island, was perfect for shipbuilding.

Shipbuilding had been known in Belfast since 1791 when William Ritchie had arrived from Scotland to establish his wooden shipbuilding industry. It is debatable, however, if shipbuilding would ever have become such a major success story in Belfast had it not been for boilermaker Robert Hickson's appointment of Edward J. Harland, who had learned his trade on the Tyne and Clyde, as his yard manager. Hickson had taken space on one of the artificial islands and had moved into iron shipbuilding in 1853. Owing to Harland's design skills and financial contacts the industry grew rapidly from having 120 employees in 1855 to 2,400 in 1870. Harland became a partner with Gustav Wolff, nephew of the German financier G.C.Schwabe who had already helped Harland buy out Hickson, and together they began the increase, through leasing, of the area of the yard from three and a half to 76 acres. Aided by the brilliant William Pirrie, they specialised in ocean-going liners and by 1900 had made the Harland and Wolff shipyard the largest in the world.

Two other shipbuilding firms had been established in Belfast in the 1860s and one of them, Workman Clark, was one of the top six in the world. Although they never competed with the 'Big Yard', as Harland and Wolff was known, they contributed to the fact that many ancillary industries were necessary. These included marine engineering, ropeworks, heating and ventilation machinery, roadworks and armaments. Shipbuilding and these associated industries required a large workforce and this led to a rapidly expanding population which in turn needed service industries and the products of food and drink companies.

As the historian, Gearoid O Tuathaigth states, when referring to the Belfast of the nineteenth century, success bred success and Belfast was the spectacular success story of Irish urban history. Although most of Ulster remained a rural economy, the area around Belfast became an integral part of the first industrial revolution in the United Kingdom and continued to prosper and increase in size. Most of the immigrants were from east Ulster and were more likely to be Protestant. There was also an influx from the rural areas and, as a legacy of the penal laws, such immigrants were usually Catholic, often unskilled and poorly paid. This led to competition for jobs. To keep pace with this population move into the city, which grew to 349,180 by 1901, there was a construction boom. This was facilitated by the freeing of building land after the dismemberment of the Donegall estates, and the availability of cheap, durable bricks. After an Act of 1847, new buildings had to have minimum standards and this led to numerous rows of small houses with tiny back yards, lavatories and ash-pits. As local sanitary conditions and health services improved, so the birth rate rose and the death rate fell. This added to the population growth and the need for more housing.

According to historians, it was at this stage, from the 1850s, when Catholics had become one-third of the population of Belfast, that religious dissension began. The Belfast Corporation was Tory- dominated and loudly proclaimed the connection between prosperity and Protestantism. Most inhabitants thought that their prosperity was due to the Union and this reinforced their support of it, and the belief in their British identity. In the second half of the century there was, according to traditional history books, a further growth in religious apartheid which was sustained by the development and divisive influence of Orangeism, the incendiary preaching of anti-Catholic clergymen, the growing nationalism of Irish politics, the Protestant resentment of the Catholic movement, the fear of home rule, the official Catholic policy of separate schools and the inequality in employment.

In a commission in 1887 Sir Edward Harland reported that of his 3,000 workers only 225 were Catholic. He did point out that they were not segregated, but it was an admission that foremen who hired and fired were invariably Protestant. This raises a further question. Did such foremen hire on religious grounds only or did they hire those who were related or known to them and were therefore, either co-incidentally, or due to settlement patterns, of the same religion? If the foremen hired purely on religious grounds, then how were 225 Catholics able to be employed? And how did this figure rise so that in 1912 it is reported that two thousand Catholics were temporarily driven from the shipyard? Whatever the answer, it is true that Protestants did monopolise most white collar occupations and had the pick of the best paid and most secure manual jobs in manufacturing and shipbuilding. This led to the strengthening of a British identity for a large part of the population.

From this time the politics and parties of Ulster are inextricably bound up with the politics and parties of Ireland as a whole. Elections were a test of strength of Irish home rule and the results established a pattern which is little changed in the present day. The Liberal-Unionist argument was that Ulster had done very well under the Union. Belfast had shown extraordinary growth, with a population which had quadrupled in fifty years and a workforce that had the highest wages in Ireland. It was the third port in the United Kingdom in terms of customs revenue and the basis of this prosperity was the economic link with Britain.

A bustling port, Queen's Bridge, Belfast 1909

(Hogg Collection, Ulster Museum)

By 1910, therefore, the north-east of Ireland contained the world's largest shipyard, ropeworks, tobacco factory, linen-spinning mill, tea machinery works, aerated water factory and dry dock. The new City Hall in Belfast, begun in 1903, was completed in 1906 and was a splendid embodiment of the technical achievements in the north of Ireland. With a large working class, an expanded middle class and a wealthy new entrepreneurial upper class, Belfast, the provincial capital, was a regional industrial city much like those in the north of England. It differed in that politics were polarised by religion and appears to have been a greatly divided city.

Before 1910 Ena O'Neill, Norman Douglas, Annie Duff, Johnny Marquis, Mary Heatherington, John Parkinson and Teresa McCallam had been born in this corner of Ireland and their births registered in the capital, Dublin.

The City Hall as it looked when just completed in 1906
(Hogg Collection, Ulster Museum)

BORN IN 1905 - ENA O'NEILL

Ena McKenna is a lady in her ninety-second year. She is clearly spoken and articulate with little apparent loss of hearing. She lives alone in a one-bedroomed flat in a sheltered housing association in West Belfast and, with the exception of a home-help for one hour per week, does all her own cooking and cleaning. Ena shops for herself though her family insists that she now goes into town by taxi instead of by bus. She also continues to decorate her home and on one of my visits she was putting a border around the top of the kitchen walls. Ena is a Catholic and attends Mass and devotions several times a week. She is deeply religious and says that when she feels a pain, she 'just offers it up.' She never takes any sort of drug and attributes her long life to no alcohol, lots of fresh vegetables and eight glasses of tepid water each day.

Ena was born in February 1905, the third child of Constantine O'Neill and Susan, nee Finn. She had two older brothers and two sisters were born after her. Unfortunately both these sisters died in infancy. Her parents were both born in Belfast, although her father's people had come there from County Tyrone. She was baptised Susan O'Neill in St. Patrick's Church in Donegal Street, north Belfast, and lived in Cavendish Street in the west of the city.

Ena's father was thirty-five years old when she was born and her mother was thirty-two. She can remember her Grandma Finn, and recalls her talking about her mother skinning rats for food during the Famine.

Ena's family home was a good-sized terrace with four bedrooms, so she never had to share a room. Downstairs there was a kitchen, parlour, scullery and pantry. The musty parlour was rarely used because her family liked to gather in the kitchen. Like the majority of dwellings in Belfast, the house was rented and Ena says that it was owned by Jews. Since it was a very old terrace, the toilet was outside and the front door opened directly on to the street.

Ena's father was the manager of her mother's parents' business, a marine chandlers, and became the owner on Grandma Finn's death. Her mother did not have to work outside the home and Ena considered their standard of living to have been quite comfortable.

St. Patrick's Church, Upper Donegall Street, Belfast c.1900.
Ena was baptised here in 1905.
(Lawrence Collection, courtesy of the National Library of Ireland)

Ena spent a great deal of time with her grandmother because her father went on frequent business trips to Dewsbury, Yorkshire, where linen merchants and marine merchants gathered, and he liked his wife to accompany him. She was enrolled in a school near her grandmother's house. When Ena was thirteen, her mother died of a weak heart, and she was sent to a boarding school in Newry where she was educated for two years. Her father employed a housekeeper, a Protestant called Mrs. Mortimer, to look after their home. When she finally left school, Ena stayed at home and did errands for her father.

In 1920 Ena's father remarried. Ena says that she was very fond of her stepmother and the half-brothers and sisters she was soon to have. In 1928 Ena's stepmother died of milk fever three weeks after the birth of her fifth child and Ena undertook the rearing of her five half-brothers and sisters aged three weeks, eleven months, two years, three years and four years. Shortly afterwards Ena married her fiance, a butcher called Tom McKenna. They honeymooned in Dublin, but not alone. The second youngest child cried so much when they were leaving that the newlyweds took her with them and she slept in a cot at the end of their bed. They continued to look after the children until they all moved away from home some sixteen years later. During this time Ena bore two daughters.

Ena's two daughters visit her regularly. Her husband died in February 1990 after suffering from Alzheimer's Disease for six years. For five of these years Ena kept him at home and 'did everything for him'. Since she is only five foot tall and weighs just six stone, this must have been difficult. Ena's weight has always been the same and she attributes her slim figure and upright bearing to having taught Irish dancing for many years. She demonstrated a reel to prove this point.

Ena has never had a full-time occupation outside the home but is an avid reader and keeps herself abreast of all local and world news. She does not describe herself as a Nationalist but she would prefer Ireland to be united because old-age pensions are higher in the Republic of Ireland and travel for pensioners is free. Ena is scathing about the 'troubles' in Northern Ireland and feels that no cause is worth a human life. She remembers the fighting in the twenties but says that then 'it was man to man, not like the present cowards who shoot men and women in the back.'

Ena's father, Constantine O'Neill, in 1910.

BORN IN 1909 - NORMAN McKEE DOUGLAS

Norman Douglas is in his eighty-seventh year. He is clearly spoken and articulate with little apparent loss of hearing. He lives alone in a three-bedroomed semi-detached house in east Belfast and, with the exception of a home-help for one hour of cleaning per week, does all his own cleaning, shopping, washing and cooking. He still drives and maintains a car. Norman is a Presbyterian who believes fervently in the union with Great Britain. He attends a local church and has sung in the choir there for fifty years.

Norman was born in east Belfast in December 1909 when King Edward VII was on the throne and Ireland was an integral part of the United Kingdom of Great Britain and Ireland. He was the fifth of six sons of Robert Douglas, who was born in Magheraknock, Ballynahinch and Elizabeth Douglas, nee Harper, who was born in Belfast. Norman's parents were Baptists, a denomination which does not believe in infant baptism, so he was not baptised.

Norman's father was an assistant foreman in the Sirocco Works, a large engineering works in Belfast, and often travelled away from home to hop-drying places such as Kent where machinery from the Sirocco Works was in use. Norman's mother did not work outside the home. He has no memory of his grandparents which is not surprising because his father was in his early fifties and his mother almost forty when he was born.

Norman was born in a three-bedroom terrace house in Ravenhill Avenue, east Belfast, and shortly moved to a substantial four-bedroom terrace across the street. Both houses had a parlour, kitchen and scullery downstairs and an outside toilet in the yard. Norman had to share a bedroom with his brother who was eight years older. There was a small garden in front of the second house and both houses are still standing today.

Norman spent his childhood in an industrial city and his father's occupation was a direct result of the industrialisation of that city. Since his father was never unemployed, they considered their standard of living to be quite good. Norman remembers being well, if plainly, fed and can recall no particular shortages. He says that, although he had nothing compared to children of today, most of the games he played cost nothing and he could get four buns for a halfpenny from the breadcarts when they returned to the Co-op Bakery in the street where he lived.

In 1923, at the age of fourteen, Norman left school and went to work in John Bell's, the photographers in Garfield Street, Belfast. He wanted to learn the trade of developing and printing, but had to leave because the place was under glass and he got sunstroke. He then went to work in an office in R.J.Allam & Son, Livestock Auctioneers, but was not happy there. After this, he was apprenticed to learn the drapery business, became a

Donegall Place in the centre of Belfast at the time of Norman's birth.
(The Lawrence Collection, courtesy of National Library of Dublin)

traveller when he had served his time and ended his working career as a director in the same company.

Norman married Greta McCausland in 1943 and, like Ena and Tom, the couple spent their honeymoon in Dublin. He has two children, a son and a daughter. In 1974 Norman became a widower; at the age of 71 he remarried and has three stepsons and a stepdaughter from this marriage. His second wife died in 1987. Norman has lived alone since his wife's death but has frequent visits from his children and stepchildren. He drives nine miles to Lisburn each Sunday to visit his daughter.

Norman Douglas has always been involved with music and was a member of a barbershop quartet in the 1930s and 1940s. He sang for the BBC in the nineteen thirties when performances went out live from the upstairs room of a house and artistes had to wear dinner suits for radio performances. He was a member of Belfast's St. Anne's Cathedral choir for many years, performed publicly in many concerts and halls around the country and once shared a stage with the famous tenor, Josef Locke. Norman drove the future prime minister, Clement Attlee, on a tour of the Antrim coast when he visited Belfast for a local Labour party conference. His boss had asked him to do this so that Mr. Attlee and his companions could drink. The morning began with a drink in the hotel and this set the tone for the day. Norman laughs as he recalls the gruffness of Clement Attlee and his terseness with words.

As a member of the Belgravia quartet, Norman was driven to war performances by Rinty Monaghan, a world champion boxer, and seems genuinely surprised that his reminiscences are of interest to me. His Dublin-registered birth, under the Births and Deaths Registration Act (Ireland) 1880, surprised him equally!

Norman is a widely read man who has a good knowledge of current affairs, reads newspapers daily and can converse on almost any topic. He is very intelligent and keeps his mind active by reading and doing crosswords. As an avid cricket fan, he goes to the cricket club to support the first eleven and to socialise. His television viewing is selective, he prefers programmes which require some thought on his part and is pleased to be able to solve conundrums on '*Countdown*'.

Norman Douglas has a keen interest in political events and can be outspoken in his views. Although he does not describe himself as a loyalist, because he feels the name has been tarnished and he is against violence, he is staunchly pro-Union. He looks upon himself as British and would not like any change in the status of Northern Ireland. Norman's attitude to the parades issue is that he thinks Orangemen should be able to march down traditional routes, but perhaps not just with the usual lodges. He says,

> 'I would like to see the Ancient Order of Hibernians walk on the Twelfth day in the parade and I would like to see the Orangemen march in the Ancient Order of Hibernians' parade. That's the way it should be. When I was a boy everybody in our street went to see the parades, but then bands were real bands and people in the lodges were dressed properly in good suits and hats.'

This photograph is of Caledon Loyal Orange Lodge and was taken some time before 1920. The men are all well dressed and have sashes, regalia and lambeg drums.

CHAPTER TWO

1910-1920: AS HISTORIANS RECORD IT

An overview of historical works for the period 1910 to 1920 would lead one to infer that there were so many crises in relation to the north of Ireland that it would have been impossible for life to have had a semblance of normality. Traditional historians have concentrated upon these major, usually divisive, events and have omitted the normal pressures and joys of day-to-day living.

George V acceded to the throne of Great Britain and Ireland in 1910 at a time when Belfast was the eighth city in the United Kingdom. Edward Carson was the leader of the Irish Unionists and the debate, on whether Ireland should have its own parliament, was raging. There was a general election in December of that year and although Asquith, leader of the Liberal Party, remained as prime minister, the Conservative and Unionist Party held exactly the same number of seats as the Liberals. Asquith was dependent on the support of 42 Labour MPs and 84 Nationalists. This meant that the passage of the Parliament Bill giving Home Rule to Ireland was inevitable. Carson needed to be sure that the unionists in Ulster were prepared to actively resist and make sacrifices. According to A.T.Q.Stewart (1967), Captain James Craig undertook to organise a demonstration to prove how serious the ordinary people of Ulster were in their plans to resist Home Rule.

> On Saturday, 23rd September 1911, 50,000 men from every part of the Province, representing the Orange lodges and Lord Templeton's Unionist clubs, marched from the centre of Belfast to Craigavon, Craig's residence on the outskirts of the city, where thousands of spectators were already gathered. Altogether it was an impressive display of solidarity by the ordinary people of Ulster.

This demonstration determined both the policy and the methods to be followed during the next three years and a 'Commission of Five' was appointed shortly afterwards. The remit of this commission was to frame a constitution for a provisional government of Ulster, 'having due regard to the interests of loyalists in other parts of Ireland.' The unionists were very serious indeed, although Winston Churchill, the home secretary, did not realise it at the time. "We must not attach too much importance to these frothings of Sir Edward Carson," Winston Churchill said in a speech at Dundee in October 1911; "I dare say when the worst comes to the worst we shall find that civil war evaporates in uncivil words."

An Ulster unionist meeting in the Ulster Hall in 1912.
(Hogg Collection, Ulster Museum)

By 1912 the *Titanic* had been launched and sunk, the Irish Women's Suffrage had been formed and the suffragist Emily Pankhurst had addressed a meeting in Belfast's Ulster Hall. Churchill was invited to speak there in February by the Ulster Liberal Association, but because of fear of unionist action, the venue was changed to Celtic Park. Five battalions of infantry had to be sent from Dublin to ensure his safety, so great was unionist hostility towards a man who wished to speak in favour of Home Rule in a building which his father had consecrated to the loyal cause and which was used as a meeting place for those vehemently opposed to Home Rule.

A further Unionist demonstration, at which Bonar Law, the leader of the Conservative party, had agreed to speak, took place on Easter Tuesday 1912 at the Balmoral Showgrounds on the outskirts of Belfast.

> Against the backcloth of the blue Antrim hills more than 100,000 men marched past the several platforms; seventy trains had been needed to bring in the provincial demonstrators, and the city's tram-car service was stopped from 8.30 a.m. until 6 o'clock in the evening.
>
> (Stewart, 1967)

Despite all these displays of strength, Asquith introduced the third Government of Ireland Bill in April 1912. Feelings were running high in the north of Ireland and in June a group of Sunday school children, on an excursion, was attacked by an Ancient Order of Hibernians procession in Castledawson. This order was a Catholic mirror image of the Orange Order and, originally formed in 1838, it had been revived by Joe Devlin who had won the west Belfast constituency for the Nationalists in 1907. The week after the Hibernian attack Catholic workers were expelled from Belfast shipyards and, in September, there was furious fighting between supporters of Celtic (Catholic) and Linfield (Protestant) football teams at a match.

On Saturday 28 September, after services in meeting halls, churches and the Ulster Hall, bands from every Protestant area of Belfast converged on the City Hall where 471,414 men and women signed the Ulster Covenant.

> In Belfast the day had been marked by exemplary conduct and sobriety. Apart from a little unpleasantness after the football match between Distillery and Celtic (and why it was allowed to be played at all defeats speculation) there were no breaches of the peace. The Times correspondent paid the city a left-handed compliment by noting that it had one of the lowest of its Saturday records for drunkenness and disorder, and the police reported that the number of arrests had been nothing beyond normal.
>
> (Stewart, 1967; Distillery was a Protestant team.)

In 1913 the Home Rule Bill was defeated in the House of Lords; the Ulster Volunteer Force (UVF) was formally instituted and was to be recruited from men who had signed the Covenant. The Irish Citizen's Army and the Irish (National) Volunteers were formed in reply. In the next year 216 tons of arms were bought for the U.V.F. and unloaded from *The Clydevalley* vessel at Larne in April.

> For almost half a century the gun had been largely absent from Irish politics and representatives had pursued their objectives by constitutional means. Now the gun had returned centre stage. The Irish tradition of armed defiance, which had seemed all but extinct, in a few short years had sprung back to vigorous life. The UVF, now impressively armed, revitalised militant separatism.
>
> (Bardon, 1992)

This arming of the UVF, following so closely on the so-called 'Curragh Mutiny', in which it was clear that army officers in Ireland would not assist in coercing Ulster, meant that :

> The 'force' option was now effectively ruled out. It was clear by mid-1914 that Ulster would have to be coerced into Home Rule, but that the British army could not be relied upon to do it.

Ulster Volunteer Force volunteers parading in the grounds of Belfast Castle in 1913. The Church of the Resurrection, now derelict, can be seen in the background.
(Hogg Collection, Ulster Museum)

The Home Rule Bill, which passed the Commons for the third time in May 1914, had allowed for opting out on a county basis but for a period of six years only. The amendment by the House of Lords had allowed for the exclusion of the nine counties, Antrim, Armagh, Cavan, Donegal, Down, Fermanagh, Londonderry, Monaghan and Tyrone, for ever. Neither formula was acceptable but both meant that partition had been, in principle, secured.

Meanwhile the Irish Volunteers grew rapidly and they had 130,000 recruits by June and weapons by July. According to Jonathan Bardon, a consignment of Mausers had been bought in from Hamburg and taken to Howth near Dublin where dozens were openly paraded on the streets by Irish Volunteers. Patrick Pearse, a founder member of the Irish Volunteers, applauded the sight of Irishmen with rifles but also wrote:

> Negotiations with the Orangemen might be opened on these lines: You are creating a Provisional Government of Ulster, make it a Provisional Government of Ireland and we will recognise and obey it.... Hitherto England has governed Ireland through the Orange lodges: she now proposes to govern Ireland through the A.O.H. [Ancient Order of Hibernians] You object; so do we. Why not unite and get rid of the English? They are the real difficulty; their presence here the real incongruity. (Foster, 1988)

World War I broke out in August 1914 and both Edward Carson and John Redmond, leader of the Irish Parliamentary Party, pledged support. The Home Rule Bill was shelved until the war would end and the 36th (Ulster) Division was formed from the Ulster Volunteers. Traditional enmities were suspended and on August 6th the following poem, composed jointly by a Belfast member of the UVF and an Irish Volunteer from the Glens of Antrim was published in the *Irish News*:

> Bless the good fortune which brings us together,
> Rich men and poor men, short men and tall;
> Some from the seaside and some from the heather,
> Townsmen and countrymen, Irishmen all;
> Ulstermen, Munstermen, Connachtmen, Leinstermen,
> Faithful to Erin, we answer her call.

There was a split in the Irish Volunteers and the first plans for rising were muted. By 1915 the Gaelic League was taken over by militant nationalists, the Irish Republican Brotherhood was reorganised and a military council formed. In April 1916 an Irish Republic was proclaimed in Dublin, followed by surrender, imprisonments and fifteen executions. Lloyd George sent Asquith to Ireland to negotiate a settlement and Carson spent an hour and a half persuading the Ulster Unionist Council to accept Lloyd George's offer of the exclusion of six northern counties. For the first time this was agreed.

On July 1st the Battle of the Somme began and 5,500 men from the Ulster Division died or were wounded in the first two days.

> In the long streets of Belfast mothers looked out in dread for the red bicycles of the telegram boys. In house after house blinds were drawn down, until it seemed that every family in the city had been bereaved. The casualty lists were full of familiar names....That year there were no Orange processions on 12 July.
>
> (Stewart, 1967)

Lloyd George ousted Asquith as prime minister in December and in February 1917 Germany launched a campaign of submarine warfare. The campaign was now a war of attrition in which the winning side would be the one that could mobilise more men and harness more economic power. Over half a million tons of British merchant vessels were sunk and the skills of the Belfast shipbuilding industry were so needed that all the workers were on overtime.

Meanwhile regiments from all over Ireland continued the long, muddy struggle and often fought side by side. On the famous battlefield of Messines, Belgium, the Volunteers of the 36th Ulster Division and the 16th Irish Division served, died and were buried together in 1917. In the following year World War I ended and it is thought that, of the 40,000 - 50,000 Irishmen who died, at least half were in all probability from nationalist Ireland, rather than unionist Ulster. News of the armistice was greeted by everyone with lively celebrations which lasted the best part of a week.

Harland & Wolff had so benefited from the need for ships during the war that they had opened a new 41 acre yard in 1917. In 1918 they launched almost twice as many tons of merchant shipping as any other shipyard in the British Isles and employed over 20,000 workers. In the same year there was republican success at the general election and by 1919 Carson had received a summons to attend Dail Eireann, the Irish Parliament. In 1920 the Better Government of Ireland Act introduced partition between two Home Rule states and there were riots in Belfast and Derry.
Catholic shipyard workers were expelled and partial martial law was in

effect in Belfast.

While all these major events were taking place Ena O'Neill, Norman Douglas, Annie Duff, Johnny Marquis, Mary Heatherington, John Parkinson and Teresa McCallam were growing up. They were living at home with their families, attending school and filling their spare time with leisure activities.

BORN IN 1903 - ANNE JANE DUFF

Annie Stewart is in her ninety-fourth year and lives alone in a one-bedroom, first-floor Housing Executive flat in east Belfast She is clearly spoken but has some hearing loss. Although Annie has a home-help for a short period each day, she still does most of her own housework and bakes for her family every Wednesday. Annie is a great-great-grandmother and goes into town to shop with her daughter every Saturday. Her daughter-in-law's mother is not very well, so Annie brings her over for afternoon tea on a Monday and bakes scones for her on Wednesday. Annie is a regular churchgoer and attends the Congregational church. She is a Unionist but does not think any political matter is worth dying for.

The new City Hall in Belfast under construction at the time of Annie Stewart's birth in 1903.

(Hogg Collection, Ulster Museum)

Annie Stewart was born in Park Avenue, Sydenham, east Belfast in September 1903 and was baptised Anne Jane Duff in the Church of St. Anne's, Belfast, on 25 September. She was the fifth child in a family of five boys and four girls. Her father, William Richardson Duff, was about forty years old when she was born but she is unsure of what age her mother, formerly Eileen Sturgeon, would have been. Annie says that when, as a child, she asked her mother her age, she always got the same response: 'The same age as that wee finger and a wee bit older than my tooth.'

Seaman Duff's little shop in Victoria Park

Long ago and what now seems to be, far away and the Victoria Park was new, a man who spent his life at sea decided to open a small shop.

Victoria Park was the chosen place as there was nowhere to buy sweets and other confections when one arrived for a day in the park.

William H. Duff, an ex-chief engineer of the S.S. Magnetic came with a very high recommendation from the Belfast Steamship Co., plus a most generous gift for his outstanding services.

His shop was small, very small, yet he served his customers well until his death. He was known affectionately as "Seaman Plum," an obvious play on his surname.

William Duff is still remembered by some of his ex-customers. After his passing, the business was taken over by 'Granda' Robinson of Derwent Street.

A larger shop replaced the tiny wooden hut and a boathouse was added with a curving wooden jetty to sit the people who wished to hire a rowing boat.

This place was the mecca of us children who made a bee-line for it after school, to be served by 'Granny' Robinson in her wee shop. We could buy all kinds of sweets, drinks, windmills, buckets, spades, balls kites and many other thing too numerous to mention.

The highight of our visit was the African grey parrot that was kept in a cage that hung from the ceiling. The children never tired looking at this bird and the more daring amongst us got manys a nip for putting our fingers through the bars.

'Granda' Robinson, as we all called him, loved nothing better than to fill his motor-boat full of kids for a trip around the park waterway and I mean the whole way round.

There seemed to be masses of boats and it was a great thrill for me when the great man himself allowed me to go out in the punt to bring in some more boats, for the waiting customers.

Alas, that beautiful parrot, that I recall so well and many people tell me they still remember, suffered a sad death from theteh fumes of tyres burning on the bonfire one Eleventh Night, as he hung in the fanlight in the hall.

The park has changed quite a bit from my young days, not so many trees to play around and no boats on the yachting pond, locally known as the "Sucking Bottle."

A local paper recalling Annie's father. She is among the girls at the front.

Annie's father had been chief engineer on the S.S.Magnetic, then he worked as a fitter in the shipyard and also had a small shop in Victoria Park. Because his name was Duff, he was well known locally as Seaman Plum. Her mother also kept a shop in the house and sold such things as sweets, matches, dummy tits, paraffin oil and camphorated oil to local people. She kept the shop open until very late at night: 'Even when she went to bed , she sometimes heard a knock and would get up in case it was somebody wanting a dummy tit because their child wouldn't sleep.'

Annie Duff's home was a rented terrace house with three bedrooms, a parlour and a kitchen, so she had to share a bedroom with her sisters. There was a large garden at the back of the house and Annie's father was a great gardener and loved to garden. The toilet was outside: 'The *[Belfast] Telegraph* was well used in them days. There was no television or anything so everybody had to buy the Telegraph to get the news. When it was read, you cut it up into wee squares and hung it up on a string in the toilet to clean your bottom with. When you wanted a wash, you went to the baths in Templemore Avenue or else took a basin upstairs so nobody else would see you.'

Annie Duff left school in 1917 and went to the weaving in the Grove factory. She had really wanted to learn how to be a dressmaker, but her family needed her wages. She hated the factory but continued there until she married William Stewart in 1926. Annie and William had a daughter and a son and when they were reared she went back to the weaving. After retiring from weaving, Annie worked in a school kitchen and as a home-help. She stopped working outside the home at the age of seventy-three.

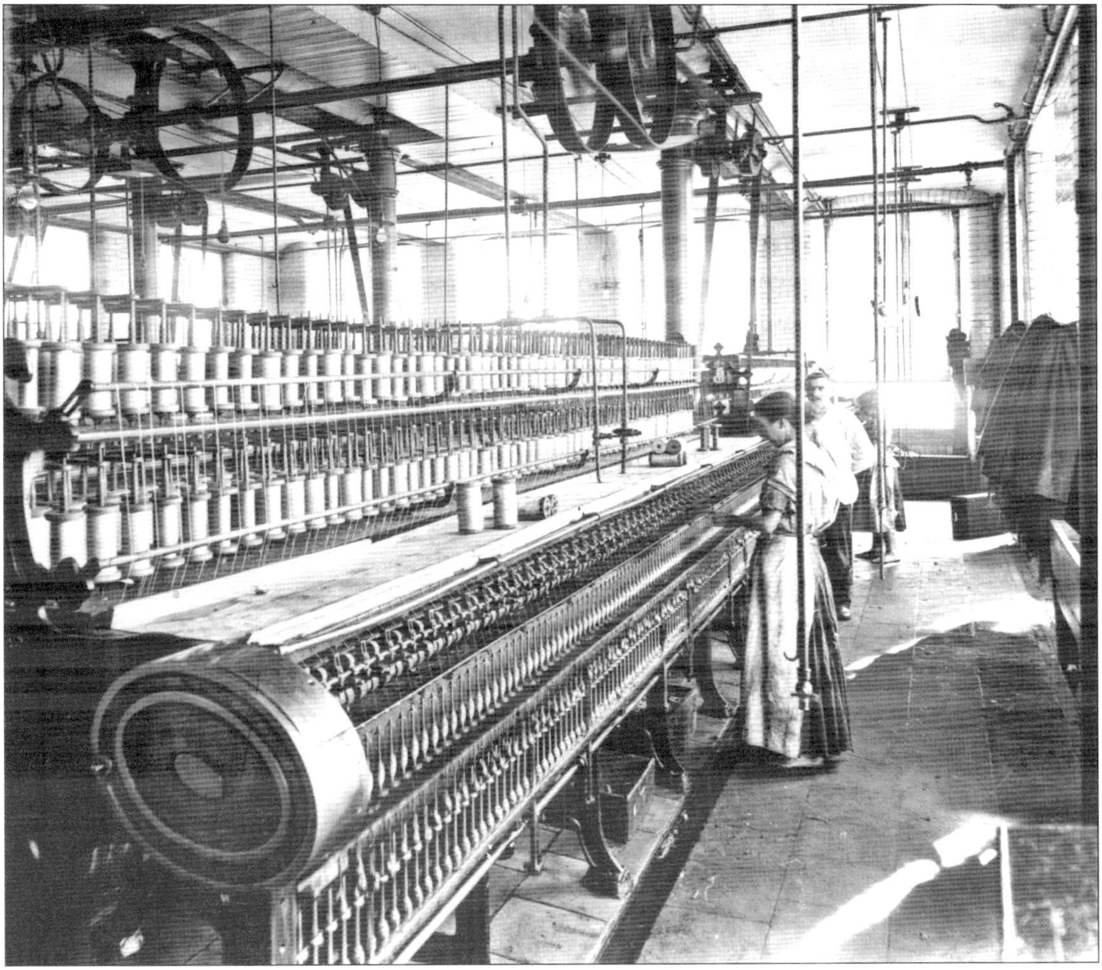

The scene inside a typical mill when Annie went to work. The woman is barefoot as this was considered safer on the wet, slippery floor.
(Hogg Collection, Ulster Museum)

BORN IN 1904 - JOHNNY MARQUIS

Johnny Marquis is an intelligent, articulate man in his ninety-first year. Since the death of his wife, he has lived alone in a sheltered housing association flat in north Belfast but has daily visits from his sons. His memory is extraordinary and he has an intense love of Shakespeare and Scottish ballads which he can quote at great length. He lives surrounded by books of learning and history and has no difficulty in completing *The Times* crossword.

Johnny was born in Ballylurgan, Randalstown, County Antrim in October 1904. He had one older sister born in September 1903, and two younger sisters, one born in March 1906 and another in May 1907, three months after the death of their father from peritonitis. Johnny's father had been a farmer and was the eldest son on a well-to-do farm. Johnny's mother had come to the farm from the Glens of Antrim to look after the family and had married his father in 1902. After his father's death, the heir to the farm became his father's brother so, according to Johnny, his mother became persona non grata. She was given money by the family to enable her to leave the farm and move back to the Glens. When she saw that her money was dwindling, she decided to move to the nearest large town, Ballymena. Johnny's mother told her children that her only skill was in looking after farmers, so she took a small house where she made meals for farmers who came into the town. Her business went well and she made a lot of money during the war which enabled her to buy a big house for use as a proper cafe in 1925.

Johnny has little recollection of the farmhouse in which he lived until the age of three. After that he grew up and shared a bedroom with one of his sisters in a two-up, two-down house in which one of the two down rooms had been converted into a cafe. He can hazily remember his paternal grandfather waving goodbye to him, and his maternal grandmother, who said she 'had never been ten miles from a cow's tail.'

Johnny was extremely bright at school and by the age of thirteen he 'was through the books' and moved from the National school to Ballymena

Academy where he did his Junior Certificate. In 1919 he went to St. Malachy's Grammar School in Belfast and from there to Queen's College (now University) where he took his degree in the same year as Michael McLaverty, the writer.

Queen's College, University Road, Belfast while
Johnny was a student there.
(Lawrence Collection, courtesy of National Library of Ireland)

Johnny then went to a teacher training college in England. He returned home to teach and met and married Kitty Cunningham. It was a long and happy marriage. Most of Johnny's teaching career was in Belfast but the happiest years he had were when he was sent to the Glens of Antrim to teach evacuee children during World War II. He said that in his heart it felt like coming home. Johnny eventually became a well-respected headmaster in the Markets, an inner-city area of Belfast.

Johnny Marquis feels that his great love of literature has meant that he could never become partisan and he could never see Ireland in isolation.

The people he mixed with during his training taught him that common humanity is what is really important. He is Catholic and would like to see Ireland united again but, he insists: 'The Scottish and English cultures are part of what has shaped Irish culture and such dimensions must be included and recognised. They are part of what makes us as we are and if we try to deny that we will lose part of ourselves. Tennyson and Shakespeare, Glencoe and Flodden, they're all important.'

Cushendall in the Glens of Antrim in 1910.
(Hogg Collection, Ulster Museum)

CHAPTER THREE
1910-1920: AS THE PAPERS REPORTED IT

Although the school-leaving age was much lower than now, and access to education was more limited, the north of Ireland contained a highly literate society in the decade before partition. In the 1911 census less than one in ten people in the nine counties of Ulster was illiterate and this figure would have been even lower for an industrial city such as Belfast. Newspapers, therefore, would have been the principal medium by which the people of the north of Ireland learned of events. It would be difficult to ascertain to what extent newspapers reflected current concerns, both political and cultural, but it must be assumed that some of what was written was an accurate reflection. It should also be remembered that newspapers in the north of Ireland, as in many other places, would have to some extent reflected their owners' political views. For this reason a variety of newspapers from the period needs be examined to discover which events people were learning of at the time.

The Belfast Weekly Telegraph of 1 January 1910 showed that people were reading about a wide range of events. The edition included 'Riotous Conduct in Belfast' and the sudden death of a County Leitrim woman, a mysterious death in Cavan, and reports of the Clones Petty Sessions and the Derry Petty Sessions. The Church News section told of 'Christmas in Dundalk' and 'Christmas in Derry'. To this day there is debate about the correct name of Ulster's second largest city with many Catholics insisting that it is called Derry, while many Protestants insist that the proper name is Londonderry, the name given to it in 1613 when jurisdiction over the city was granted to the city of London. There was apparently no confusion in 1910 when all papers referred to the city as Derry. Furthermore, the geographical area on which the paper reports is not limited to Belfast or the nine Ulster counties and reports on the Dublin Cattle Market and Ireland's potato industry were included on page 12.

On 8 January 1910 the same paper did include political news, but it was merely reported as a newsworthy event and no editorial comment was made on it. Page 2 had a large heading 'Nationalism' and underneath is a report on Tim Healy, an Irish MP, and his scathing speech in Dundalk, while page 10 had a large notice 'Irish Unionism' giving details of a Belfast demonstration. This issue also told of forthcoming events, such as a concert in St. Enoch's, Belfast, and Children's Cinderella in the Ulster Hall. Advertising was confined to entertainment with the exception of an advertisement offering 100 acres of government land free for farming in Canada. The lead article on page 4 reflected some of the strict evangelical views which prevailed at the time. It was entitled 'Are Whist Drives Wicked?'.

Throughout the year all the issues of the *Belfast Weekly Telegraph* reported the news in the same provincial way with local issues i.e. the area around Belfast to the fore, then events in the nine counties of Ulster, then news from the rest of Ireland and finally English and world news. We read of 'Wm. Bridgett and Sons, Ireland's Greatest Banner Painters in Great Victoria Street, Belfast' (2 July 1910), of a death sentence which had been passed in Limerick, (9 July 1910), and the success of 'Irish medical students, Samuel Wright from Belfast and John Hegarty from Dublin, in Scotch examinations' (30 July 1910). English news in the 3 September issue includes the death of Florence Nightingale on 13 August and the arrival of the murderer Dr. Crippen in London on 27 August. At no point was there any indication that the editors at any time envisaged the partition that was to occur only ten years later.

The spread of the suffragist movement was taking place in Belfast just as in other large cities. On 30 July 1910 there was a report of an 'At Home' in Holywood for Miss Gladice Keevil, a non-militant suffragist from London. It was described as a 'brilliant gathering'. Mrs. Pankhurst's address on 13 October attracted an even larger audience.

There was a Women's National Health Association of Ireland and the members gathered in Coleraine on 12 February to hear a lecture on infant mortality. In the Bachelor of Arts results in July we read of four second class passes in Modern Languages. All were women. However, as the following advertisement indicates, some issues relating to women were still a rather cloak and dagger affair!

> Married Lady has marvellous valuable information;
> priceless value for ladies; beneficial,
> - Mrs. Arons, Elizabeth St., Liverpool.
> Enclose stamp. Mention paper. B5485
>
> 22 October 1910

'Catch-My-Pal', an anti-drink movement, started at this time and in Belfast the evils of drink was one of the topics fervently preached upon all over the city. In December Mrs. Booth-Clibborn, eldest daughter of General Booth, founder of the Salvation Army, came to Belfast and, according to the *Belfast Telegraph* on 10 December 1910, opened a 'most successful two-weeks' mission in the People's Hall, York Street'. This was only one of many missions which took place throughout the year.

Newspapers also gave statistical information and in the issue of 5 November there are details of the annual death rate, which was registered in Dublin. These figures show that the death rate in 1910 per 1000 population was 4.5% in Lisburn, 8.4% in Newry, 13.7% in Armagh and 16.0% in Belfast. What is interesting about these figures is that, first, the registering of them in Dublin reiterates the fact that Dublin was the capital, and that, secondly, the death rate in Belfast was so much higher than less industrialised areas. The causes of death in Belfast are also listed and they show that pneumonia was the greatest killer, closely followed by phthisis (tuberculosis) and then diarrhoeal diseases.

The results of the election in 1910 are reprinted in the issue of 10 December and confirm the political divisions that would increase as the decade progressed. They also confirm the settlement patterns of the time in Befast, some of which are unchanged in the present day.

ELECTION RESULTS IRELAND

Belfast (South)		Belfast (West)	
Chambers (U)	5585	Joseph Devlin (N)	4543
Sloan (I.U)	2722	Sir John Smiley (U)	4080
Down		Louth	
J.Craig (U)	4110	R.Hazelton (N)	2509
J.Williamson (Lib.)	2412	T.M.Healy (Ind.N)	2021

Monaghan	
J.C.R.Lardner (N)	3365
M.E.Knight (U)	1937

For leisure activities there are reports throughout the year on a wide variety of events and no event is reported as having any particular religious affiliation. In February the Belfast Shakespearean Society presented 'Hamlet' in the Ulster Minor Hall and there was a 'Hunt' in east Antrim. In July races took place at Inishowen, Co. Donegal, cricket at the Victoria Cricket Club, Belfast, golf outings in various location and a meeting of the Archaeology Society. Gold Plate cigarettes were three pence for ten and 'At the club, at the bar, at the buffet, everywhere, Dunvilles Three Crowns Liquer'[sic] was advertised as the thing to drink.

A reading of the history leading up to 1910, and the dramatic historical events of the decade itself, would make one expect that contemporary materials of the years 1910-1920 would reflect a great polarisation in Belfast society. An examination of some newspapers of the time does not confirm this expectation. In the *Belfast Weekly Telegraphs* of 1910 people would have learned almost nothing that to us today would be called 'sectarian', and in studying those papers now there is little to be found that would indicate a divided society. What differences there were seem to have been treated humorously and show a tolerance of prejudice as the following extract from page 3 of the *Belfast Weekly Telegraph*, 1 January 1910, aptly demonstrates.

Riotous Conduct in Belfast

Mr.N.Tughan, a Belfast solicitor, in the Police Court on Monday had to defend a man who had been openly cursing the Pope in the Falls Road. The prisoner, Thomas McKinstry, was charged with drunkenness and riotous conduct, and Constable Conroy said that he lay on his back on the road and loudly cursed the Pope.(Laughter) There was a hostile crowd round him.
Mr.Tughan - Do you know any person outside a lunatic asylum that would go up the Falls Road and do anything of that sort? (Laughter)
The Constable - I don't think so.
- He was not far from the asylum? (Laughter)
- He was on the direct road for it. (Laughter)
Mr.Tughan confessed that when he received instructions in the

case from the man he did not know what plea to put forward except the plea of insanity from drink. His client had not been up for thirteen years previously.

The insanity plea did not avert the inevitable 40 shillings penalty.

As the author, Lynn Doyle, writing at the time, said 'we are conscious of our bitterness and see the ridiculous side of it now and then. In a strange way it is a bond of union.'

The great shipyard of Harland & Wolff symbolised the industrial wealth in the north-east of the island and newspapers frequently reported the orders, trials and launches which kept 14,000 men in employment. No orders were greeted with more enthusiasm and pride than those from the White Star Line for three of the biggest ships in the world, the *Olympic,* the *Titanic* and the *Gigantic.* By 31 May 1911 the *Olympic* was undergoing sea trials and the *Titanic* was prepared for launching, an event well covered in the newspapers.

LAUNCH OF THE TITANIC

Impressive spectacle at the Queen's Island

In the presence of thousands of spectators, the *S.S.Titanic,* which will share with the Olympic the distinction of being one of the two largest vessels afloat, was launched from Messrs. Harland and Wolff's yard at the Queen's Island yesterday.... The clanging of hammers was heard all over the ship as the preparations for the launch were developed, but the men using them were for the most part hidden from view. On the deck of the boat the figures of the workers whose duty it was to see to the drag ropes and cables were dwarfed and blurred by the distance which separated them from the people down below. About twelve o'clock Lord Pirrie left the owner's stand in order to make a last tour of inspection and to give final instructions.... Over the bows of the vessel the White Star Company's flag floated, and there was displayed a code signal which spelled the word "success". If the circumstances under which the launch took place can be accepted as an augury of the future, the *Titanic* should be a huge success....

Belfast News Letter 1 June 1911

The launch of the Titanic in May 1911.
(Hogg Collection, Ulster Museum)

Success was not to be the fate of the *Titanic* . Amid much publicity the biggest and most luxurious ship of the time sailed from Belfast on 2 April 1912 to Southampton, England, then to Cherbourg, France, before making her final stop in Queenstown, Ireland. From there she headed for New York and on 14 April 1912, under the command of Captain Edward J. Smith, she hit an iceberg in the icy waters of the north Atlantic and sank within two and a half hours. Of the 2,208 passengers and crew on board only 705 were rescued. Although designed to carry forty-eight lifeboats there were only sixteen, and two collapsibles on board. This sinking on her maiden voyage brought sadness to all citizens of the home of her creation.

BELFAST FEELING GLOOM IN THE CITY OF THE LEVIATHAN'S BIRTH

In a special and grievous manner did yesterday morning's terrible tidings of the *Titanic's* foundering in the waste of ice-strewn water off the coast of Newfoundland strike home to the consciousness of the community in Belfast. It is not too much to say that every citizen experienced the sensation of reflected glory when the *Titanic* took her place amongst the great ocean going leviathans, and felt a certain satisfaction in being at all associated with the city which witnessed the production of the world's largest vessel. How the sentiment of civic pride was aroused by this triumph of talent and toil so auspiciously launched from the Queen's Island.

Remembering this it is easy to understand that a very real feeling of public sorrow was created in Belfast by the series of Marconigrams [transatlantic wireless telegraph service invented by Marconi and used by the navy from 1907] in yesterday morning's newspapers which set forth bluntly and coldly the story of the *Titanic*.

Irish News 17 April 1912

The departure and subsequent sinking of the *Titanic* was one of two major topics with which newspapers in April 1912 were filled. The debate regarding Home Rule was raging and all newspapers carried stories of the nationalist rally in favour of the motion. On 1 April 1912 the *Irish News* had a two-page spread on the pro-Home Rule demonstration in Dublin under the headlines 'We Will Have Home Rule, Mighty National Demand From Great Dublin Muster.' This muster was described as attracting half a million people and the newspaper stated that every religion and every citizen interest was represented. There were 'thrilling scenes of fervour' and 'Mr.Redmond, leader of the Irish Parliamentary Party, prophesied that the Home Rule Bill would be passed.'

Less attention was paid by the *Irish News* to the anti-Home Rule unionist demonstration which took place on Easter Tuesday, 9 April 1912 in the Balmoral Showgrounds in Belfast. Beforehand the newspaper did publicise the event as the 'Balmoral Blow Out' and urged that 'the people who want to protest against native government must do it in a sensible way.' Questions were asked in Parliament about the drilling which had taken place in the weeks before the demonstration and some comments were quoted in a light-hearted fashion.

> Mr.McVeigh: 'In a speech a few days ago Lord Dunleath said that it is not military drill, but squad drill, and that the only object is to enable the large body of Orangemen to turn around when they receive the word of command from their leader.' (Loud laughter)
>
> *Irish News* 2 April 1912

On the day after the demonstration, it was reported in the same newspaper as the 'Bonar Law Meeting at Balmoral' that was 'not as impressive as the Dublin muster.'

At the Balmoral demonstration, organised by the Ulster Unionists, Orange Lodges and Unionist Clubs joined together to show their opposition to Asquith's Home Rule Bill. They were addressed by Andrew Bonar Law, leader of the British Conservative Party.

(Hogg Collection. Ulster Museum)

The memorial to the local victims of the *Titanic* disaster as it looked when first erected in Donegall Square North on 25 June 1920. The names were inscribed in order of importance and the list was headed by Thomas Andrews, the ship's designer and nephew of Lord Pirrie. The ceremony was performed by the Lord Lieutenant of Ireland, Field Marshall Viscount French, and music was provided by the band of the Royal Irish Constabulary.

The acceptance of the Home Rule Bill in Westminster warranted four full pages of coverage in the *Irish News* on 12 April and the complete text of the bill was printed on 18 April. The tragedy of the *Titanic* continued to be given ample coverage and the opening of a relief fund for relatives of those drowned was well advertised.

Sporting events and entertainment also attracted a lot of attention in April 1912 and were uninterrupted by the Home Rule debate. With no acrimony the (Protestant) Belfast Blues played (mixed) Distillery in Grosvenor Park and gave all proceeds to the Belfast Maternity and Mater Infirmorum Hospitals. Cinemas had extra Easter programmes and The Grand Opera House advertised a change of programme in the *Irish News* so that readers would come and 'watch our King and Queen through India.' One event attracted great attention:

Buffalo Bill's Wild West Shows
President Col. Wm. Cody
Are Coming to Jones's Road Grounds Dublin
From April 15th - May 15th
400 Red Indians (Different Tribes)
800 Cowboys & Cowgirls
2000 Horses
Animals of all Descriptions
With Various Side Shows
Excursions from all
PARTS OF THE COUNTRY
OTHER PARTICULARS LATER
WATCH AND WAIT
LOOK AND WONDER

Forthcoming Easter holiday breaks filled the advertisement columns, with many combined rail and hotel coupons available. Four nights in Rostrevor (forty miles from Belfast) cost forty-four shillings and included rail fare, hotel and all meals. Excursions to Portrush, Derry, Ballycastle and Bundoran were also a popular feature.

GREAT NORTHERN RAILWAY
(IRELAND)
EASTER HOLIDAYS
on THURSDAY 4th APRIL
A Special Train will run from Belfast
to Bundoran at 10.15 a.m.
Return Excursion Fares

1st Class	2nd Class	3rd Class
17/-	13/-	9/-

Irish News 3 April 1912

Extra sporting activities took place around the Easter period although the wettest and windiest Easter Monday in memory spoiled the planned 'Grand Balloon Ascent and Parachute Descent.' The point-to-point races at Ballyhaft, outside Newtownards, attracted large crowds. In football Glentoran defeated Cliftonville and Belfast Celtic beat Distillery in the 'New Irish Cup Competition', and there was an Irish international victory when Ireland defeated Wales by three goals to two.

Theatres and cinemas were filled to capacity during the holidays and many had extra showings of 'thrilling dramas' such as 'The Corsican Brothers', 'The Mermaid', 'Stolen Treasure' and 'The Cow Boy Pugilist'. Other amusements also had crowded houses and many flocked to the Empire to hear 'Tom Jones, The Welsh Harry Lauder'. The West Belfast Temperance Flute Band made its first public appearance and provided 'the very best music, a real and pleasant surprise to the people of the Falls and surrounding areas'. (*Irish News* 5 April) As a temperance band the musicians would have played without the help of 'Ireland's Best Whiskey, SHAMROCK,' which was 'distilled in Belfast by Kirker Green and Company'.

The West Belfast Temperance Band may well have preferred 'Ross's Belfast Dry Ginger Ale', being advertised here in the *Illustrated London News* in 1912.

By this time the cinematograph had arrived in Belfast and over the next few years its popularity would grow rapidly.This applied not only to picture palaces such as the Kelvin Picture Palace, which had opened in 1910, but to other establishments. McQuiston Church (east Belfast) , like other Belfast churches, was in the forefront of showing films to the populace. This enterprise was known as 'Pleasant Saturday Evenings for the People' and was inaugurated in McQuiston on 9 November 1912. The Story of the Belfast Central Mission describes similar events in the Grosvenor Hall where they had 'Saturday Happy Evenings' which included the performance of musical works by famous composers as well as cinematograph.

Newspapers were the major means of advertising entertainment and an examination of issues of the newspaper *Ireland's Saturday Night* in 1913 confirms the large number of cinemas and theatres which were offering 'amusements' in all areas of Belfast .

Alexandra Theatre :	*Little Red Riding Hood*
St. Georges Hall:	Vitagraph dramas
Panopticon Exhibition:	Tom Thumb - 23" tall
Grand Opera House:	Shakespeare: A Different Play Each Night
Alhambra:	*The Triumph of Strength*, Pit 2d, Lounge 4d, 6.50, 9.00.
Palladium:	Ireland's Representative Comedian Chalmers Mackey.
Coming next week -	*The Wearing of the Green*
Grand Opera House:	Peter Piper, Prices 6d - 3s.
Theatre Royal:	Mr. Stanley Carlton's Company in the Sensational Drama, *At the Price of his Life* 3d - 1s.
Empire Theatre of Varieties:	The Six Gordons in Comedy Vocal & Dancing May Newell - the popular Soprano Grand cinematograph and vocal entertainment every Sat.

Central Picture Theatre (Smithfield) : continuous 2 - 10.30
Younita or *From Gutter to Footlights*

Royal Hippodrome :
twice nightly - Ella Shields, The Cycling Buffoons

Kelvin Picture Palace :
Great feature film by Kalem - *Retribution*

The Kelvin Picture Palace, College Square East, c.1911. This is the earliest known photograph of a Belfast cinema.
(Hogg Collection, Ulster Museum)

In sport there was an even greater variety of events advertised and reported upon throughout 1913 and they indicate thriving leisure activities which catered to all members of the community. The *Nomad's Weekly* of 28 January 1911 stated that a match played by one of the five league teams in the city of Belfast could draw a crowd of 10,000 and these supporters would have been of both religious persuasions. The first issue of *Ireland's*

Saturday Night in 1913 showed a picture of such an event, the 1 January George Willis Benefit Match between Linfield and Belfast Celtic. On 25 January Glentoran (Protestant) played Celtic II (Catholic) at the Oval and Linfield and Celtic I met. On 5 November Scotland played Ireland at Celtic Park and the match was advertised as having 'The cream of Scotch and Irish players.' These football players would obviously have been from all over Ireland. Football was not provincial; teams played in the Irish Football League and matches between Glenarm (Antrim) and Bohemians (Dublin), Shelbourne (Dublin) and Distillery (Belfast) were advertised in the same issue (1 November 1913).

Apart from football, many other sports were advertised. These included dog racing at Celtic Park and Lambeg, trotting in the Royal Ulster Agricultural Society Showgrounds, the annual meeting of the Ulster Anglers' Association, the National Cross Country Championships, rifle shooting, a badminton international between Ireland and England in Dublin, racing at Windsor, boxing at the 'Star', and notes regarding chess clubs, gymnastics and athletics. (1 February 1913)

On 21June there was an advertising notice of the Athletic Carnival to be held by the North Belfast Harriers in Celtic Park and in the athletics section there was a report which stated that 'The Irish Amateur Athletic Association has selected the following team to represent it in the annual international contest against Scotland on Saturday, 19 July.' This team again included athletes from all over Ireland, e.g. in the 100 yards F.R.S. Shaw from Dublin and S. McComb from Belfast were both taking part.

Other popular sports which warranted sections in the same paper were bowling, yachting, hockey, rowing, cycling, motor cycling, marksmanship, golf, cricket, angling, boxing, whippet racing, model yachting and pigeon racing. In the section Homing Pigeon Chat, the number of clubs listed indicates how widespread and popular the sport was, as well as the fact that it was participated in by people of both religions. They included North Belfast, South Belfast, West Belfast, Avoniel, Ballymacarrett & District and Mountpottinger Homing Pigeon Societies.

In 1914 there was a plethora of leisure activities for the people in the north of Ireland. As well as sporting events, there were theatres, music halls, picture houses, restaurants, fish and chip shops, pubs and Italian ice-cream parlours with bright lights and gramophone music. Rising incomes and the emergence of a skilled working class created new possibilities, and entertainment became an industry which catered to all sections of the community.

The popularity of gramophone music led to regular advertisements being placed in the *Belfast Telegraph*.

Even in the middle of World War I this business of entertainment continued. A study of the *Belfast News Letter* and the *Irish News* of 1916 reveals some of the entertainment possibilities during that year. *The News Letter* is a paper whose readers would have been mostly of the Protestant religion, while the *Irish News* would have been read principally by Catholics, and yet many of the same venues are advertised in both papers.

On 3 April 1916 advertisements in the 'Amusements' column of the *Irish News* included ones for the Clonard Picture House, the Hippodrome, the Empire, the Alhambra, the Panopticon, the Coliseum, the Imperial, the Central and the West Belfast Picture Theatre. In other issues the *Irish News* carried advertisements for Belfast Musical Competitions in the Ulster Hall and a Great Ulster Attraction, A Night in Venice in the Ulster Hall.

It is worth noting that these events were taking place in the hall where Lord Randolph Churchill, thirty years earlier, had urged loyalists to organise against Home Rule and which was associated with this in the minds of unionists.

The Shakespeare Tercentenary Celebrations, under the distinguished patronage of their excellencies the Lord Lieutenant and Lady Wamborne and a lecture by the Right Hon. W.S.M. Starkie Litt.D. [father of the Romance scholar Walter Starkie] in the Assembly Buildings were also advertised in the *Irish News*. (26 April) Those who placed the notices must have considered that the events would have been of interest to the Catholic readers.

The *Belfast News Letter* advertisements were mostly for the same picture houses and music halls as those advertised in the *Irish News*. In September The Harmony Four and the Yamagata Japanese Troupe were appearing at the Hippodrome while Sunshine and The Star Variety Company could be seen for 4d to 1sh.2d at the Empire. The Duncairn Picture Theatre, 'Belfast's Super Cinema', was showing *The Devil's Brew*, and *The Eternal Grind*, featuring Mary Pickford, was being shown at the Imperial Picture House, while The Imperial Symphony Orchestra rendered 'Appropriate Music to the Pictures'.

The Royal Hippodrome, a popular theatre which opened in 1907.
(Lawrence Collection, courtesy of the National Library of Dublin)

On 8 September both the *News Letter* and the *Irish News* urged readers to go to the Hippodrome to see:-

The Biggest
& Best of all Revues
Joy-land
The Last Word in Beauty Choruses
100 Joy Belles   4d - 1sh. 8d

The Grand Opera House in Belfast presented a mixed programme of entertainment from 1895 and advertised in all newspapers.
(Lawrence Collection, courtesy of the National Library of Dublin)

Sport in 1916 was little affected by war and many similar events were advertised and reported on in all newspapers. In the *Irish News* there were items about Dog Racing in Celtic Park, the Irish Cup when Glentoran met Linfield at Grosvenor Park, the Annual Sports at Ballymena which included horse-jumping and trotting, Gaelic Athletics, the Newmarket Meeting (England), the Punchestown Meeting (County Kildare), an 'Enjoyable Afternoon with the East Antrim Hounds', and the Charity Cup where Belfast United met Belfast Celtic and Distillery played Cliftonville on 12 April. The semi-final of the Charity Cup was advertised on 14 April on page 1 of the *Irish News* and highlights the normality of Catholic teams playing Protestant teams, as well as the esteem for the armed forces.

Tomorrow
Charity Cup
Semi - Final Tie
Linfield v Glentoran at Grosvenor Park
Belfast United v Distillery at Cliftonville
Admission 6d & 9d
Ladies 6d to Reserved
Soldiers and Sailors 6d to all parts

On Easter Monday, 24 April, while buildings in central Dublin were being seized by Irish Volunteers, the paper advertised The Gold Cup in which Cliftonville played Linfield at the Oval and Glentoran played Glenavon at Windsor Park. In the County Antrim Football Association Dunmurry Rangers (Protestant) played St. Peter's Swifts (Catholic) and in the Irish Intermediate League Celtic 2nd played Glentoran 2nd without incident. On the same day there was a 'Record Easter Monday Meeting' at Celtic Park where whippet racing and trotting were taking place, and a large golf tournament at Royal Portrush Golf Club.

Sporting reports in the *Belfast News Letter* were also from all over Ireland and in September included steeplechasing at Dunmore, racing, cricket, football and bowling, a report on the Sligo horseracing and Cork Park racing. Cricket was widely reported on and the following advertisement, found on page 1 of the 7 September edition, indicates no difficulty with the nationality of the players.

CRICKET
AT ORMEAU TODAY, AT 11.30 SHARP
ENGLISH BOYS V IRISH BOYS
(Under 14 years of age)
Admission, sixpence

At no point does either the *Irish News* or the *News Letter* make any reference to religion when reporting sporting events and the only sport which is in the *Irish News* and not in the *News Letter* is Gaelic Football. The spread of Gaelic sports was being encouraged at the time and in the *Irish News*, 24 April, there was a report on the G.A.A. Congress with the headline 'Progress of the National Games in Ulster; Most Rev. Dr. MacRory's Support for Hurling.'

Other leisure time events in the *Irish News* in 1916 included advertisements to 'Dine at the XL Restaurant in Corn Market', for a meeting of the Children's Aid Society for Ireland at which 'The chair will be taken at 3.30 p.m. by the Right Rev. Professor Hamill, Dr.D, Moderator of the General Assembly', to attend Holy Week Services and to holiday in the Four Courts Hotel in Dublin. The *News Letter* recommended staying all over Ireland: in Killarney, 'The Most Beautiful Spot in the Kingdom', the Recess Hotel in Connemara, the Lough Swilly Hotel in Buncrana, the Great Northern Hotel in Bundoran or, as advertised by the *Irish News*, the Four Courts Hotel in Dublin.

Unlike the present day, amusements and advertisements were reported on page one in both the *Irish News* and the *News Letter* and sporting events were on page two. Local news was reported on pages three and four and included 'An Interesting Co. Fermanagh Slander Action' which was being prosecuted in the Dublin Law Courts; the proceedings at the Spring Graduation Ceremony in Queen's University at which the Vice-chancellor admitted that the experiment on 'The Admission to Full University Privileges of women in common with men' had succeeded; the Belfast Stock Exchange prices (under a heading 'Irish Stocks and Shares'); and a 'Defence of the Realm Charge' in Derry .

News and advertisements from all provinces of Ireland were included in both newspapers and the editors of the *Irish News* and the *News Letter* obviously considered that they would be of interest to readers of both religions. Some examples of this in the *News Letter* in 1916 were: sales by auction of Roscommon, Galway, Cheviot and Wicklow sheep in the Dublin market, Dublin Law Reports, a notice that the Stewart Institution for Imbecile

Children and Hospital for Mental Diseases in Palmeston, Co. Dublin, 'receives backward or imbecile children from all parts of Ireland', a Dundalk bankruptcy matter, a Donegal tragedy, an Armagh murder trial and a Tyrone probate.

The Easter Rising in Dublin was reported in the *Irish News* in a factual way and only the editorial imparted any opinion :

> We have passed through one of the saddest and most deplorable weeks in our nation's history.
> Knots of misguided young people were induced to emulate the example set them in the Capital.
> It is needless to dwell upon the hopelessness, the mad folly, the blind fatuousness of this reckless adventure.
>
> (1 May 1916)

In 1916 war news took up a large portion of both papers, although it was obviously not policy for newspapers of the period to put 'news' on the front page. The *Irish News* reported war news on pages three and four and the *News Letter* used pages five and six. Both papers displayed an equal interest in the war which reflects the fact that both had readers whose families were involved. On 1 April 1916 the headings in the *Irish News* were: 'The Zeppelin Raid', 'The Russian Front', 'Mr. Asquith in Rome', 'Another German Crime', 'Red Cross - Queen Mary's Appeal'.

In September the *News Letter* recorded the total casualties for August - 4,693 Officers and 123,097 men - and listed those in the Royal Irish Fusiliers who had died:

> Brady, 21767, J. Dublin
> Coyle, 15252, N. Belfast
> Gattney, 3070, L.Cpl.J., Corryrock, Monaghan
> McKernan, 20950, P. Belfast,
> Maguire, 30805, J. Dublin

No religious division was reflected in war reporting in either newspaper and there was no evidence in the *Irish News* of any anti-war propaganda.

There were as many reports there as in the *News Letter* and even the advertising had a patriotic flavour.

KEATINGS POWDER
SEND YOUR SOLDIER BOY A TIN
IT KILLS BEETLES, BUGS,
FLEAS & BODY VERMIN

Irish News 1 April 1916

By 1918 the war had exacted a huge toll from the people in Ireland and still many events continued as usual. The following contemporary report, reprinted in the Falls Community Council History Project, demonstrates how, two years before partition, sporting fixtures between Protestant and Catholic teams could take place without acrimony.

> The Irish Cup of 1918 proved to be a very tightly fought contest. As yet, Celtic had never won the Cup and the final with old rivals Linfield proved to be as tough and uncompromising as ever. The Final ended in a 0-0 draw and the replay was scheduled for Cliftonville on Saturday 13th April. Prices were an unusually expensive 2s for reserved enclosure and 1s for unreserved.
> Just before the match began, 'a very faithful impersonation of Charlie Chaplin, get-up, dander, and whirling cane, cigarette end etc, toddled on the field in approved Chaplin style and presented Mick Hamill with the usual decorated horseshoe. He had a hearty ovation.'
>
> The horseshoe didn't prove of great value to Celtic, because despite playing a 10-man Linfield for most of the second half, Celtic failed to score and the result was another 0-0 draw.
>
> The second replay was set for Wednesday April 24th at Grosvenor Park. The notice announcing the match added that 'extra time will be played if necessary.' Kick-off was at 6.45 p.m. and in front of 15,000 fans and in beautiful summer weather, Celtic tried to break

the two-match deadlock. Celtic: 2 Linfield: 0 When the game ended the crowd chaired Hamill and Stewart off and a great crowd wanted the Celtic players outside the grounds.

Happily the entire match was free from any incidents of crowd violence.

The entertainment columns of newspapers in 1918 show how widespread was the continued popularity of music halls, theatre and cinema and the types of entertainment which were attracting customers from all walks of life.

IMPERIAL.
TO-DAY.
"THE NARROW TRAIL."
A Super-Production in Five Acts, by the Artcraft Corporation, featuring WILLIAM S. HART.
Supported by
THE FURTHER EXPLOITS OF JUDEX.
Episode No. 4, in Two Parts:
"THE ROOM OF A THOUSAND SNARES."
"THE FLOORWALKER."
A Splendid Two-part Comedy, featuring CHARLIE CHAPLIN.
And Full Programme of Exclusive Features.
Continuous Performance—1-0 to 10-30 p.m.
Imperial Symphony Orchestra 3-0 to 5-0 and 7-0 to 10-30 p.m.

POPULAR PICTURE PALACE.
NEWTOWNARDS ROAD (City End).
6.50—TWICE NIGHTLY—9.
TO-NIGHT.
"THE LAW OF THE LAND" (5 Parts),
Starring OLGA PETROVA.
BOB ROBINSON and PARTNER.
In "The Old Cobbler."

LYCEUM. 6-30 to 10-30. Wed. and Sat. at 4
THURSDAY, FRIDAY, and SATURDAY.
Frank Keenan in a remarkable Triangle drama,
"THE HEART OF A MAN."
W. S. Hart in a real Western "gripper,"
"HORNS AND HOOFS."
Episode 7 of Pathe's Master Serial,
"THE SEVEN PEARLS,"
And Full Programme.

DUNCAIRN SUPER-CINEMA.
Five—"THE LITTLE DUCHESS"—Reels.
Starring
LITTLE MADGE EVANS.

KELVIN PICTURE PALACE.
THURSDAY, FRIDAY, and SATURDAY
"THE TRIALS AND SORROWS OF TORQUATO,"
The Shakespeare of Italy
(In Four Reels).

WILLOWFIELD PICTURE HOUSE.
TO-NIGHT.
"BOOTLE'S BABY."
London Film, from the celebrated Comedy Drama

HIPPODROME
6.40—TWICE NIGHTLY—8.45.
MISS ETHEL WARWICK and CO. in
"A WOMAN INTERVENES."
W. H. PROWSE. MIKE NONO.
WIN and WINDLE.
THE KORAHS.
THREE DORISE GIRLS. FRANCO.
FOUR CLOVELLY GIRLS.
Prices 4d to 2s. Booking, 10 till 3; Saturdays, 10 till 1.

EMPIRE. 6-45—TWICE NIGHTLY—8-45 'PHONE 832.
JOHN LAWSON
Supported by Lucille Sydney and Strong Supporting Company, in
"THE LITTLE BROTHER."

ALHAMBRA TO-NIGHT. 6.50—9.
"THE MAN TRAP."
A Blue-Bird Masterpiece, Thrilling and Gripping
(In 5 Reels), starring Herbert Rawlinson.

PICTURE HOUSE,
LARNE.
GIGANTIC ATTRACTION.
October 24, 25, 26.
SECURED EXCLUSIVELY AT ENORMOUS EXPENSE,
THE OFFICIAL WAR PICTURES,
"OUR BOYS IN FRANCE."
From the Base to Going Over the Top.
WONDERFUL SCENES OF
THE IRISH GUARDS,
THE ROYAL IRISH RIFLES,
THE ROYAL IRISH FUSILIERS,
THE ROYAL MUNSTER FUSILIERS,
And other Irish Regiments at work and Recreation.
FINE SHOW OF TANKS.
THE FINEST FILM OF THE IRISH IN FRANCE EVER PRODUCED.
Come and see this Picture. You are sure to recognise some of your Friends.

Belfast Telegraph, October 1918

There seems to have been no problem with nationality in Larne! In fact cinema-goers in Larne would have been watching at the same time as those in Bray where 'Our Boys in France' was also being screened. The film was so popular in Rathmines, a Dublin suburb, that it had to be retained for a further three days.

THE
PRINCESS, RATHMINES.

OWING TO SPECIAL REQUEST.
WE HAVE DECIDED TO RETAIN
THE FILM
" OUR BOYS IN FRANCE."
FOR A FURTHER THREE DAYS
UNTIL SATURDAY.

SCENES OF THE DISASTER TO THE
R.M.S. " LEINSTER."

BROADWAY JONES,
featuring George M. Cohan, the American Comedian.

BILLIKEN COMEDY.
NEW PATHE GAZETTE.

PEARL WHITE, in "THE FATAL RING."

PROFESSOR RENAUD'S FAMOUS ORCHESTRA.

The *Irish Times*, October 1918

The *Irish Times*, published in Dublin, reported events in Ireland and Britain in a manner similar to the papers printed in Belfast. On page one of its 24 October 1918 edition there is a roll of honour for the war dead and advertisements for businesses all over Ireland such as Millar and Beatty, Grafton Street, Londonderry, P.O'Reilly Ltd., Dublin and Belfast and the Ireland and England Royal Mail Service. There is also a notice of a Grand Red Cross Pageant entitled 'From The Battlefield to Blighty' which was to be accompained by a military band, the bands of the Royal Irish Constabulary and the Dublin Metropolitan Police.

Irish recruiting figures are given and show that, even at this late stage of the war, young men from all parts of Ireland were still willingly enlisting. For the period 1 June - 23 October the total for all Ireland was 10,650. It was broken down as:

Belfast	3,976	Limerick	571
Dublin	2,485	Armagh	355
Omagh	955	Mullingar	342
Waterford	790	Galway	234
Cork	763	Sligo	179

On the same pages there are reports on the annual meeting of convocation at Queen's University Belfast and the overwhelming vote in the House of Commons, 274 - 25, to adopt a resolution expressing 'its desire that a Bill shall be passed forthwith making women eligible as Members of Parliament.'

Many notices and advertisements are identical to those in Belfast papers.

THE SEAMEN'S CRUSADE

Will you please help us to collect

£50,000

Remember

FRYATT. CAVELL.
LUSITANIA. LEINSTER.

OUR OBJECTS ARE:

1. To Boycott the Huns after the War until they have made full atonement and reparation for their crimes against humanity, including the cold-blooded murder of **15,000** non-combatant sea-faring men.

2. To assist the patriotic Labour to counteract the Bolshevik, Defeatist, and Pacifist influences which are helping the enemy.

Will YOU not help ?

The Bolshie Bosses have plenty of money and they are asking for another £100,000.
We cannot believe that we shall appeal to patriotic Irish Men and Women in vain.

NO DONATION TOO SMALL OR TOO LARGE.

J. HAVELOCK WILSON,
Merchant Seamen's League,
49 St. James's Street, London, S.W. 1.

Irish Times, *Belfast Telegraph*, *Belfast News Letter*. October 1918

War reports are given in the *Irish Times* with such headings as 'Great Battles of the Scheldt', 'A Steady Advance - Irish Troops in Africa', 'Mr. Balfour and the German Colonies' and 'Armistice Terms.' World War I was drawing to a close and the correspondent from the headquarters of the British Army in France gave his view for the readers.

> ... in the near future the British troops will be beyond any line of French soil they have yet trodden in this war. It is the infantry who are carving out this victory - battalions from the English shores, the Scottish heather, the Welsh hills and the soft emerald levels of Ireland.

The Irish Recruiting Council continued to appeal for volunteers from the whole country.

You want Peace with Honour!

Will Peace bring Honour to You?

Peace—when it comes—will bring **Honour** to all who have fought to **Win** it!

Peace of Mind will be with those who have borne the **Burden of Battle!**

Peace will bring **Permanent Dishonour** to **All Fit Irishmen** who have held **Aloof!**

Volunteer now and help to bring **Lasting Peace** for Posterity and ensure **Peace of Mind** for **yourself.**

Irish Recruiting Council,
Grand Central Hotel, Belfast,
also Ballymoney, Ballymena,
Lisburn Banbridge, Newry,
Newtownards, Downpatrick,
etc.

In some instances the juxtaposition of advertising and news reports highlights the fact that war and peace were both part of life in the decade.

THESE ARE THE MEN WE TALK PEACE WITH.

HUN FIENDS AND PRISONERS.

BELGIANS PLACED IN RED-HOT VICE.

The German Government protests against the reproach of illegal and inhumane actions made against the German land and sea forces, and thereby against the German people.—The new German Note.

The Belgian Minister of Justice has now issued a further report on the atrocities committed by the Germans against Belgians in Belgium and against Belgians taken to Germany as prisoners.

All the facts have been investigated, and are vouched for by the Judicial Committee of Investigation.

Here are a few examples from Hun camps:

OSNABRUECK—Some prisoners of war who refused to work in a coal mine were placed between two bars of red-hot iron forming a gradually closing vice of fire.

HOLZMINDEN—Four or five prisoners were shut up in a dungeon, tied to posts, and left in that position for several days. The posts were gradually heated by means of radiators up to an unbearable temperature.

MINDEN.—Forty prisoners were subjected to the same torture for eight days. Their food consisted of bread and water, except that every fourth day they were given soup.

MUNSTER (Westphalia).—Another prisoner was kept for thirteen days in an overheated drying-room, and given bread and water only. He recovered from the effects after forty-two days in hospital.

At another camp a number of prisoners were tormented with hunger food was placed on a table guarded by a strong party of soldiers, who promenaded the prisoners round the tables and prevented them touching any food until they had consented to do their allotted work.

At Soltau a prisoner was tied to a stake for 24 hours without food.

Another prisoner was tied to a high post, and two large paving-stones on which he was standing were removed, and he was left suspended in the air. He was unconscious when cut down.

At Gottingen the commandant dealt with prisoners who refused to work as follows:—They were placed in a tiny barbed wire enclosure from which there was no escape. The ground was hollowed out so that a permanent pool was formed. The unhappy men who were left in there for 48 hours could only sit or lie down in water.

The general acting as Governor of the Province of Hanover caused the following rules to be enforced at the camp of Steinhorst against men who failed to work:—

First Refusal—Three days' solitary confinement without food.

Continued Refusal—Solitary confinement without bed coverings; 10ozs. of bread for three days, ordinary diet on every fourth day.

Further Persuasion—Butt-ends of rifles may be used up to the point of forcing voluntary work.

Last Resort—Prisoners may be shot by order of an officer or warrant officer.

TO-DAY, FRIDAY, SATURDAY.

THE ARGYLE CASE

Thrilling Seven Act Film

THE story of "The Argyle Case" is that of the mysterious murder of John Argyle, a multi millionaire, in the library of his home. Circumstances point strongly toward Argyle's adopted daughter, Mary, who is the beneficiary under his will, Argyle having quarrelled bitterly with his son, Bruce. Just as things begin to look black for Mary, Asche Kayton, a great private detective, is called in by Bruce and takes hold of the investigation. His methods are both scientific and swift and the trail leads to a den of counterfeiters where by the use of the dictograph and other modern devices the real murderer is run to his lair. From the moment when Kayton takes hold of the mystery the story intensifies in interest, working up to its surprising climax in the den of the counterfeiters.

Orchestral Music

THE PICTURE HOUSE

ROYAL AVENUE, Belfast.

Page 6, *Belfast Telegraph* 24 October 1918

At the end of the war later in the year all papers reported the joyful celebrations. On 12 November the *Irish News* headlines reflected the happy mood and told of Local Rejoicings, Great Public Festivity and London Celebrations. The Armistice holiday was also recorded and schools and technical institutes advised of the closure. There was little evidence in the papers that a divided country was imminent. Decommissioning in Ulster attracted almost as much column space as Home Rule.

ULSTER VOLUNTEERS' ARMS.

In the House of Commons yesterday Mr. Dillon asked the Chief Secretary whether he would state where the arms of the Ulster Volunteers now are, and in whose custody they are; whether any conditions were attached to their surrender, and if so what these conditions were.

Mr. Shortt—I have nothing to add to the reply given on the 15th inst. to a question on this subject by the honourable member for the College Green Division (Mr. Nugent).

Mr. Dillon—I would like to ask has your attention been drawn to the fact that in Ireland an impression is widespread that there has been no genuine surrender of the arms at all?

Mr. Shortt—There are a great many opinions widespread in Ireland at present. (Laughter.)

Mr. Dillon—Is the right honourable gentleman aware that a great deal of mischief has been occasioned in consequence of this impression? Are we to understand you to decline to answer my question—whether any conditions have been attached to the surrender of these arms, and if so what the conditions are??

Mr. Shortt—I have stated the conditions already.

Mr. Dillon—No, you have not.

An Honourable Member—Have the arms been surrendered by the Nationalist Volunteers,

Mr. Shortt—I understand they have been substantially surrendered.

Mr. Dillon—No, they have been taken by force.

HOME RULE AND CONSCRIPTION.

Questions in Parliament.

CONVENTION STILL SECRET.

In the House of Commons yesterday, Mr. Pringle asked whether the Chancellor of the Exchequer could inform the House whether the Committee engaged in drafting a Home Rule Bill had reported to the War Cabinet, and whether the House would have an opportunity of considering the result of its deliberations.

Mr. Bonar Law—I think the honourable gentleman has already asked me that question, and if he asks me the same question every day I must give the same answer: I have nothing to say on the subject.

Mr. Pringle—There is a change in the situation.

Mr. Shortt, in reply to Mr. Byrne, said he must refer the hon. gentleman to the reply he gave on Tuesday with regard to the question of the advisability of withdrawing the conscription proposals for Ireland.

Mr. Byrne—Will the right honourable gentleman, on taking into consideration recent events, say whether conscription is still a war necessity, or whether it will be enforced for political reasons to injure Ireland? ("Oh, oh.")

Mr. Shortt—I have nothing further to add.

Mr. Clancy asked the Chief Secretary whether the regulation made under the Defence of the Realm Act, under which certain documents relating to the proceedings of the Irish Convention might not be published, had yet been repealed; if not, what was the reason for refusing to repeal it, especially in view of the fact that a general desire has been expressed by the members of the Convention for the publication of the documents, and if he would now consider the advisability of facilitating the immediate publication of the documents referred to.

Mr. Shortt—I have taken the opinion of the members of the Convention, and they are not unanimous. On consideration, I have come to the conclusion that the regulation should not be repealed at present.

Mr. Clancy—What proportion of the members of the Convention objected to its repeal?

Mr. Shortt—I cannot speak accurately from recollection, but a large majority are in favour of repeal.

Mr. Hugh Barrie—Have you received a unanimous request from the Unionist members of the Convention in favour of the repeal?

Mr. Shortt—I have received a request—whether unanimous or not I cannot say.

Just as much attention was given in this issue of the *Belfast Telegraph* to Dublin's Chamber of Commerce sending congratulations to Marshal Foch and a private conference on the League of Nations attended by Church leaders of every denomination.

CONGRATULATIONS FOR MARSHAL FOCH.

At yesterday's meeting of the Dublin Chamber of Commerce, the president, Mr. E. H. Andrews, D.L., proposed—That "the Dublin Chamber of Commerce desires to convey its hearty congratulations to Marshal Foch, Commanding the Allied Forces, and to the gallant troops under his command, on the magnificent victories which they had achieved, and trust that their efforts will not be relaxed until the German menace has been destroyed for all time." He thought that every member of the Chamber who had been reading the news during the last few weeks felt that they, as Irishmen and as members of the great British Empire, owed this vote of congratulation to the great General who had been in supreme command of the armies which had recently been making such magnificent progress in France and Flanders. Mr. Crowe seconded the resolution, which was passed.

THE CHURCHES AND THE LEAGUE OF NATIONS.

A private conference consisting of representatives nominated by the responsible heads of Christian Churches was held at the Central Hall, Westminster, on Wednesday. The purpose of the conference was to consider the advisability of early united action by the Churches in support of the League of Nations proposal. After careful discussion the following resolution was adopted, to be forwarded to the Archbishop of Canterbury:—

"This meeting, comprising representatives of the Church of England, the Roman Catholic Church, the Baptist Union of Great Britain and Ireland, the Congregational Union of England and Wales, the Presbyterian Church of England, the Primitive Methodist, United Methodist, and Wesleyan Methodist Churches, realising the responsibility of the Churches in reference to the speedy furtherance of the League of Nations proposal, respectfully requests the Archbishop of Canterbury to summon a gathering consisting of the heads of all the British Churches, together with other representatives by them appointed, to confer without delay, and to appoint a standing committee to take appropriate action in support of the League of Nations proposal."

In December 1918 newspapers were greatly concerned with the General Election and rallies were widely reported. Sport and entertainment, however, continued uninterrupted by political events. Mixed religion football matches were still taking place and on Christmas Day the *Irish News* reported that Glentoran played Distillery at the Oval, Cliftonville played Celtic at Grosvenor Park and Linfield played United at Windsor Park. The same edition also reported on racing, steeplechase, coursing and trotting. Throughout 1919 the only interruption to such events was the large workers' strike. The *Belfast Telegraph* reported on racing at Newmarket, golf, billiards, boxing, rugby, trotting, coursing on 1 October, 'a great sports meeting in Celtic Park in aid of the Belfast Moulders who are on strike' on 5 December, and a gigantic boxing programme at the Oval on Boxing Day at which one could see the 'Cream of English, Scotch and Irish Boxers.'

Even after the end of World War I, and in the last two years before partition, there was, therefore, still little evidence of division in the advertising of leisure pursuits and no distinction in the reporting of events from all areas on the island of Ireland.

Meanwhile Ena O'Neill, Norman Douglas, Annie Duff, Johnny Marquis, Mary Heatherington, John Parkinson and Teresa McCallam were reaching the end of their school careers and were not to know that they would soon have a new capital, a new Prime Minister and a new government.

BORN IN 1908 - MARY JANE HEATHERINGTON

Mary Jane Thompson is in her eighty-ninth year and, although not very mobile, still lives alone in her own terraced house in east Belfast. She has had two operations to try to repair a broken leg and they have left her dependent on her family and carers, who come to her home several times a day. She is extremely articulate and keeps herself alert through reading and watching television and videos. Mary needs help to get in and out of bed each day but, at eighty-eight, still managed to travel to England to spend two weeks with one of her daughters.

Mary's parents were both from County Tyrone where her father, George Heatherington, served his time as a wheelwright in a sawmill in Clougher. The mill was owned by people called McKeown who were cousins of Mary's mother. After serving his time, Mary's father, aged twenty, married her mother, Sarah Jane Graham, and they travelled all over Ireland to wherever there was work. Their first child, Mary's older brother, Willie, was born during a spell in Wexford where Mary's father had managed to get a job doing repairs on a big estate. The family then moved to Belfast where an uncle dealt in cattle and pigs near Andersonstown. He found the family a house to rent in Clondara Street off the Falls Road and it was here in May 1908 that Mary Jane Heatherington was born.

During the next ten years the family moved around in search of work and two more sons and a daughter were born. They lived in some fourteen houses in Belfast, Saintfield, Holywood and Portadown and Mary says not two of them were born in the same house. Matthew was born in Saintfield, Tommy in Holywood and Ruby in Strandtown in Belfast.

All their houses were small and Mary usually shared a room with her brothers. The toilets were outside and in one house, in Portadown, there was no running water: 'You had to go to the well for water. I'd a wee blue can and my father had a bucket. I still can picture my father taking me by the hand. We passed a woman called Essie; she used to sit outside her own cottage door with a big spinning wheel in the good weather.'

The Heatherington family in 1919. Matt, George, Tommy, Willie, Ruby, Sarah and Mary. 'There was a terrible 'flu epidemic that year and my father thought it was dreadful that, if one of us died, we wouldn't have a picture of us all together. We were all dressed up and taken to Abernethy's for a photograph. I was eleven.'

Although Mary's father could build a wheel from beginning to end, he did all different jobs when work was scarce, usually in housebuilding. Later in life he started up a building business of his own and the family settled in east Belfast where they attended the local Church of Ireland church, St. Mark's. 'My sister was baptised out of the same cup as the famous writer, C.S. Lewis, and my father knew his father. He often talked about Lewis of Littlelea.' Mary's mother, who was a bit older than her father, was kept busy rearing five children and moving house. She never complained about the upheaval and would have moved anywhere her husband wanted.

Mary Heatherington left school at the age of fourteen even though she had passed the scholarship examination with honours. She is proud that one of her brothers did continue his education: 'You didn't think of going on in those days, especially since I was the eldest daughter. My older brother was going on to be a chemist and that was more important. Eventually he opened his own chemist's shop.' She went to the Technical college at night to learn business studies with shorthand and typing and started work in S. Moore's, a provision merchants. 'It was high class, yet I remember rats out at the back of the shop and the pork being cut off to the knuckle where the rats had chewed on it. I had ten shillings a week to start and I worked from 8.30 to 6.00 on Monday and Tuesday, 8.30 to 1.00 on Wednesday, 7.30 to 6.00 on Thursday, 8.30 to 6.45 on Friday and 8.30 to 9.00 p.m. on Saturday. We got half an hour for tea then and sometimes I walked home afterwards to save the tram fare.'

On one of these walks home, Mary met her future husband when he followed her home and asked her out. They had a happy marriage with two daughters and three sons. Mary's daughters now live in England and she is well cared for by her three sons. Her younger brother and sister are alive and Mary is pleased that, despite her own lack of mobility, her brother and sister are still driving their cars.

BORN IN 1907 - JOHN PARKINSON

John Parkinson is an alert and articulate ninety year old who lives with his sister-in-law in a detached house in south-east Belfast. His wife died thirteen years ago and he is visited often by his three sons and grandchildren. He celebrated his ninetieth birthday with a large family dinner party in a local hotel. John's hearing and memory are excellent and he leads a very busy life. He is the President of the Ulster *Titanic* Society, never misses a meeting, and represents the society at functions and conferences. He is very proud of the fact that his father worked in the shipyard, Harland and Wolff, and was engaged in the building of the *Titanic*. His father's tools are still in his possession and he gives excellent talks to schoolchildren about the *Titanic* and the times he saw the great ship. I attended one of his talks and he kept the eighty children present spellbound. John has been a lifetime member of the Boys' Brigade and is involved in their old boys' group, the Stedfast Association, which he attends regularly.

John was born in Belfast in January 1907 and named after his father Francis John Parkinson. He was the second of four children and had an older sister and two younger brothers. His mother and father married late in life and his father was fifty when John was born; his mother was several years younger. Both his parents worked before they married, his father as a joiner in the shipyard and his mother in the mills. Although his parents were from Belfast, there was some family connection with Lisburn and John has kept the receipt for a large family grave in Lambeg near Lisburn. He describes it as having a wonderful Connemara marble headstone and being three breadths wide. In 1887, when purchased, it cost £65.

John Parkinson was born and spent the first twenty years of his life in a terraced house in Distillery Street, off the Grosvenor Road in west Belfast. The house was owned by his family. Some years before his grandfather, who had a grocery business, bought four houses and a shop in the street and these had been left to John's father. The house had two bedrooms, an outside toilet, and opened directly on to the street. The family had the rent from the other houses as well as John's father's income, so had no financial problems.

John (standing) with his sister, Aggie, and brothers,
Jim and Stanley, in 1915.

John attended the local National school until the age of twelve. He then sat an entrance examination for the original Belfast Model school on the Falls Road. 'This model school was a wee bit select and you had to sit an entrance exam to get in, and you had to pay a fee of five shillings a quarter. I was twelve when I got in so I had two years there.' When it was burned down after partition John asked to leave school and go to work in the shipyard. His father agreed on condition that he went to the technical college at night. He started in the shipyard as a message boy because he was only fourteen and his apprenticeship as a joiner could not begin until he was sixteen. He stayed in Harland and Wolff for sixteen years and kept his promise to his father to go to the Tech at the same time. He then went into teacher training and became a woodwork teacher.

When war broke out in 1939 John was teaching unemployed boys in a training school. The school closed down so he went to work in Short and Harland's aircraft factory as an inspector. When the war ended John returned to teaching, this time in a secondary school in south-east Belfast.

John is widely read and can converse on many topics. He describes himself as a strong supporter of the union with Great Britain. He is very opposed to violence and fails to understand why people cannot live in peace with each other.

BORN IN 1909 - TERESA McCALLAM

Teresa Marlowe is an extremely sprightly eighty-seven year old whose eyes twinkle with delight as she talks. She is very articulate and has an excellent memory. She lives alone in her family home in Portaferry, County Down and takes care of the house without help. This means carrying in coal and lighting her coal fire each morning. Teresa's niece does the shopping for her and volunteer workers look after a part of her half-acre garden. Teresa is a Catholic who attends Mass regularly. She loves to travel and does so often. Her last journey was on a pilgrimage to France which she found 'a bit exhausting'.

She was born Teresa McCallam in October 1909, the eleventh child of Patrick McCallam and Mary, nee Treacy. At the time of her birth two of her brothers had already died, aged eighteen and twenty. Her father was forty-nine and her mother was about forty when she was born in Portaferry. Teresa describes how they came to live there: 'My mother was from Glenravel and my father was born in 1861 in Ballycastle, County Antrim. My mother came to work in Belfast in Bishop Dorrian's house where she helped the footman to serve at the table. My father was a teacher in St. Malachy's in Belfast and he stayed at the bishop's house. That was how my mother got to know him. She was supposed to be going to Dublin to work, but my father wouldn't let her go and, even though she was only about nineteen, he asked her to marry him. They were married on 24 June 1886 in St. Patrick's in Donegal Street.

Shortly afterwards my father took ill and the doctor said he would have to move out of Belfast. They went first to Rasharkin, County Antrim, where he had a temporary teaching position, then he was given a choice between Carnlough and Portaferry. They chose Portaferry because they thought it would be better for Patsy, their first baby. Her next ten children were all Portaferry people and she often talked about the fact that she had to pay ten shillings for the nurse when other people had to pay only five shillings. My mother said that they thought she had money because she was the schoolmaster's wife, yet, in reality, she had only one ten shillings paid when she'd to start gathering up for the next one. There was a man, Johnny, lived away at the end of the road and he was talking about my mother to me and he said: "I'll never forget the day your mother arrived in Portaferry. She came in a long car. I was down the town whenever the long car came in and the young schoolmaster got out. I'll never forget her, such a lovely young woman. I can tell you what she had on; a lovely pale gray costume and a pale gray hat with a lovely pink ostrich feather in it. I watched them come to help her out of the long car with the infant in her arms. One thing I never forgot was her lovely auburn hair." Until Johnny told me that I never knew my mother had auburn hair. To me her hair was a fairish colour but that's because auburn people don't turn gray.'

The motor bus in Portaferry before 1916. This bus operated from Newtownards to Portaferry. Was this the 'long car' that brought Teresa's parents to their new home?
(W.A. Green Collection, Ulster Folk and Transport Museum)

Until the age of three Teresa lived in a cottage along the shore and her father taught in the local school earning £8 a quarter. He coached extra pupils at home at night to supplement his income and provide for his large family. In 1913 Teresa's father died as the result of an accident when he fell into a ditch on his way home from tutoring late at night. The family had to move to a labourer's cottage with three rooms, an outside toilet and no running water. During the next four years two more brothers and a sister died from tuberculosis and yet Teresa remembers it as a happy home with lots of visitors. 'You loved visitors and there was never anybody turned away. There was a great big double bed in the room off the kitchen, that's the biggest room, and we knew when people were coming to stay because the pillows were put down at the bottom of the bed and you never knew whose head your feet might be touching. The house was always full, especially when there were visitors, and there never seemed to be any shortage of those.'

Teresa did well at school and won a scholarship but she could not take it because her sister, Brigid, got married. The duty of staying at home and looking after her mother became Teresa's. Her only regret is that she would have loved to have been a doctor.

Teresa McCallam married in 1948 but sadly she is now widowed. She keeps busy by reading a lot, doing crosswords ('the harder the better') and knitting. She likes to watch only current affairs programmes on television and describes herself as curious and interested in everything. As she talks her sense of humour and enjoyment of life shine through. Teresa loves having visitors, especially her nieces, enjoys all church events and says she would travel on outings anywhere.

CHAPTER FOUR

1910-1920 AS PUPILS LEARNED THROUGH IT

In 1831 the Irish National school system had been established and the main aim stated was to 'unite the children of different denominations'. However, by the end of the century the overwhelming majority of Irish schools were under denominational control, even though they were financed chiefly by the state. There was an unpaid Board of Commissioners which had complete control over textbooks. Reading books for five different grades, texts on arithmetic, geography and agriculture were published under the auspices of the Board. Progression through a school was denoted by the book a child was 'on'. These reading books contained a great deal of factual material rather than imaginative fiction, and lessons on English grammar, natural history, political economy, geographical material and biblical stories were featured.

In 1872 the system of payment by results was introduced and, although it was abolished in 1899, the Board at this time ceased to issue books at public expense, so many of the textbooks which had been issued by direction of the Commissioners during payment by results remained in the schools. From 1900 a 'Revised Programme for National Schools' was adopted by the National Board and the new Resident Commissioner, Dr. W.S.M. Starkie. As well as reading, writing and arithmetic, this revised programme included kindergarten, manual instruction, drawing, singing, object lessons, elementary science, physical education, cookery and laundry which were all obligatory. However, because of lack of sufficient funds, science, cookery and laundry were not widely available. The outbreak of World War I increased the financial problems and so, until partition, texts used were either old ones issued under the auspices of the Board or the very few new ones which schools could afford to buy. Since more than sixty percent of schools before 1920 were single-teacher schools, new purchases would have been minimal.

According to P.J. Dowling, a writer on Irish education, the fact that nearly all schools were denominational at this time was not necessarily a negative thing since it meant that 'the religious convictions of each child were fully safeguarded' although, unlike elementary schools in England, 'no religious emblem or pious picture was permitted in National schools'. He insists that there were always friendly relations between Catholic and Protestant teachers and 'it was known that on occasions the Protestant headmaster of a National School received the thanks of a Catholic bishop for giving religious instruction from Catholic textbooks to Catholic children attending his school - the only school within reasonable distance from their homes'.

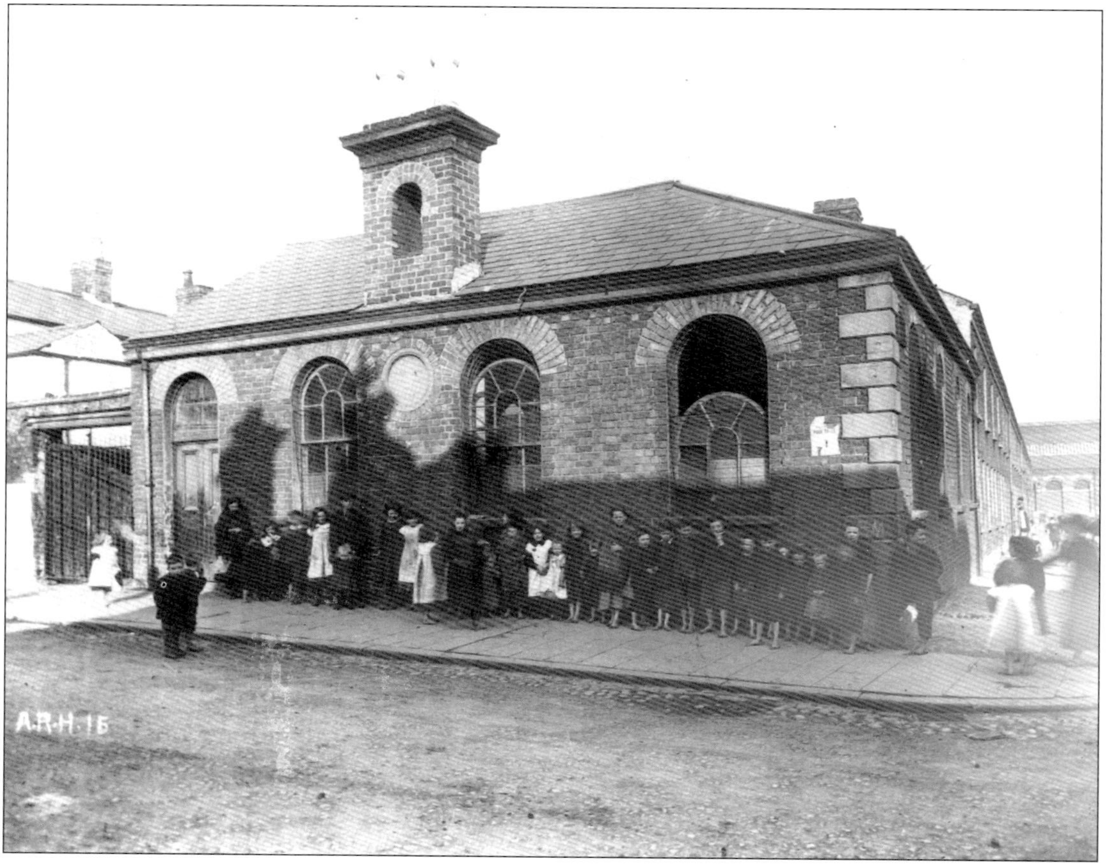

Conway Street National School, off Falls Road, Belfast, in 1902.
(Hogg Collection, Ulster Museum)

Not all schools were National schools before 1920 since there were many under the control of religious and charitable organisations. Such schools had to help raise their own funds.

Christian Brothers Bazaar.

GRAND CARNIVAL AND FÊTE

AT

ULSTER GROUNDS, ORMEAU ROAD,

ON

WEDNESDAY & THURSDAY Next,

Sept. 6th and 7th.

Formal Opening by ALEC. WILSON, Esq., J.P., on WEDNESDAY, at 3 p.m.

NUMEROUS ATTRACTIONS.

Pierrots, Half-hour Dances, Whist, Bowling Competitions, Aunt Sally, Clock Golf, &c., &c.

R.I.C. BAND WILL ATTEND.

ADMISSION, 6d. - - CHILDREN, 3d.

Belfast News Letter
5 September 1916

The following report on this Christian Brothers' Bazaar, copied from the *Belfast News Letter* of 7 September 1916, indicates that Dowling's assertions were correct and there was little ill-will towards schools of other denominations. The article also highlights the fact that fundraising for a school of one denomination was assisted by many from other denominations.

Christian Brothers' Jubilee Carnival and Fete Interesting Opening Ceremony

A grand carnival and fete, promoted in aid of the forthcoming Christian Brothers' Jubilee Bazaar, was opened in the Ulster Grounds, Ballynafeigh, yesterday and will be continued this afternoon and evening. The object of the bazaar is to raise the sum of £7,000 to help on the work of the five schools in Belfast under the control of the Christian Brothers , and considering the prominence given to questions of education in recent times, especially since the commencement of the war, it is certain that the movement will receive a large amount of public sympathy and support. The idea of the carnival and fete was happily hit upon as a lucrative means of augmenting the proceeds, and no pains were spared by those at the head of affairs to make the project as remunerative and enjoyable as possible. The chairman of the Executive Committee is Mr. J.J. McDonnell, J.P. and the vice-chairman Mr. W. Kilmartin, while Mrs. Smith acts in the capacity of treasurer, and Mrs. Carney and Miss Macauley perform the duties of honorary secretaries. In addition to the parade of cyclists in character, numerous amusements have been organised with a view to increasing the revenue, and these include roulette, football board, Big and Little Willie, Aunt Sally, hoopla, clock golf, shooting range, wheel of fortune, Black and White, and an open pairs bowling competition. The band of the Royal Irish Constabulary, under the direction of Mr. George C. Ferguson, is in attendance and supplies a pleasing variety of musical selections. Lord and Lady Pirrie wrote wishing the promoters success in their undertaking, and hoping all the friends in Belfast would contribute generously and help them out of their present difficulties....

Mr. A. Wilson, J.P., who was received with hearty applause, said he took it personally as a great compliment that one of the greatest institutions in that great and progressive city should have asked him to take part in the proceedings....

Those schools had held an important and useful position in this city for fifty years past, and the present was the first occasion on which those responsible for the schools had come before the public and asked for support..... they should all stand together and see that the appeal was successful.

An examination of some of the textbooks used in schools before 1920 provides some evidence of what was being taught to children who were at school at that time. Reading books were indeed very factual and demonstrate the theory of the time that learning to read should be combined with increasing one's knowledge. One of the *Century Readers*, published by Blackie and Son of London, Glasgow and Dublin , with a 'Price to Pupils in National Schools of five pence', is filled with stories, poems and dictation exercises which are all factual in content. One story called 'Jack and Kate' tells of Jack Brown's first geography lesson about the sun and the stars and is obviously aimed at eight-year-olds. It begins:

> Jack Brown's face was bright with smiles as he ran along to school. It was just three weeks after his eighth birthday, and that morning he was to have his first geography lesson.

The story is then followed by a poem for the children to learn and it is designed to reinforce the facts learned.

> Whether fair, whether foul,
> Be it wet or dry,
> Cloudy time or shiny time,
> The sun is in the sky.
>
> Gloomy night, sparkle night,
> Be it glad or dread,
> Cloudy time or shiny time,
> Stars are overhead.

Geography textbooks of the period provided outline maps of the countries of the world with important information, such as the capital, rivers, mountains, size and population of each one. Details of Ireland are provided in one section. In *Sullivan's School Series, Modern Geography,* published in Dublin in 1899 the following was given in the section on Ireland:

> Its length from Fair Head in Antrim to Mizen Head in Cork is about 300 miles.
> Its breadth from Howth Head in Dublin to Slyne Head in Galway is about 170 miles.
> Population - 4,700,000
> There are four provinces subdivided into counties.
> They are Ulster, Leinster, Munster, Connacht.
> Ulster has nine counties.
> Belfast, the capital of Ulster, is one of the most prosperous cities in the United Kingdom.

Longmans' Shilling Geography, published in London in 1889, has the same information in a more detailed form. In one copy, with the inscription 'H.F.Gallager, St.Colman's College' on the flyleaf, there are further examples of what was being taught -

> Ireland is the second island in point of size of the British Islands, and lies to the West of Great Britain.
> Ireland is divided into four great provinces, viz. Ulster, Leinster, Munster and Connacht.
> Ulster : Towns: Belfast, on Belfast Lough, 200,000 inhabitants, cotton and linen manufacturers, distilleries, shipping and shipbuilding.
> Leinster : Towns: Dublin, the capital of Ireland.

History was not one of the obligatory subjects in National Schools but the number of textbooks from the period before partition attests to the fact that it was a subject in many schools. One such textbook was *The Combined Irish and British History Reader,* printed and bound in Ireland by Blackie & Son, Belfast and Dublin. The copy examined had the inscription

- E. Adeline McKeown, Glenavy N.S., Aug. 30th 09, Ireland. 'Part IV, From 1700 - Modern Times' gave an outline of the Irish history being taught at that time.

Irish History

1. Dean Swift 1
2. Dean Swift 2
3. Growth of the Popular Party in the Irish Commons
4. The Volunteers
5. Henry Grattan 1
6. Henry Grattan 2
7. The Independent Irish Parliament 1
8. The Independent Irish Parliament 2
9. The French Revolution
10. The Rebellion of 1798
11. The Union of the Parliaments
12. O'Connell and Catholic Emancipation 1
13. O'Connell and Catholic Emancipation 2
14. The Famine of 1847
15. The Irish Land Acts
16. Education in Ireland 1
17. Education in Ireland 2

An extract from 'O'Connell and Catholic Emancipation', in this textbook, demonstrates the general tone and politics of the Irish history which children were learning:

> The Duke of Wellington shrank from the horrors of a civil war in his native country. He feared that O'Connell might either lead the Irish people into rebellion, notwithstanding his peaceful protestations, or that the excited people might break loose from his control. In a long speech in the House of Lords he declared: " I am one of those who have passed a longer part of my life in war than most men; and if I could avoid even one month of civil war in the country I love so well, I would give my life in order to do it."

> These noble words, coming from the greatest man in Britain, had their effect on the entire nation. The prejudices of the illiberal and the fears of the ignorant melted away.
> The year 1829 saw, in the person of O'Connell himself, the first representative in the British Parliament professing the Roman Catholic religion since the days of the last Stuart king.

Another history textbook of the period, *A Concise History of Ireland*, was published by The Educational Company of Ireland Ltd. in 1920 and was an abridgement of a longer textbook published in 1909. It dealt with the history of Ireland from earliest times to 1908 and is in six parts.

PART 1	The manners, customs, and institutions of the Ancient Irish
PART 2	Ireland under Native Rulers
PART 3	The Period of the Invasion 1172 - 1547
PART 4	The Period of the Insurrection, Confiscation and Plantation
PART 5	The Period of the Penal Laws
PART 6	The Modern Period

This textbook ends with a postscript written by the author, D.W. Joyce.

> Matters are gradually improving year by year; and those who have the welfare of the country at heart entertain strong hopes that the time is not far off when the people of Ireland will at last be prosperous and contented.

There had been little evidence of prosperity in this 1902 picture of Springfield National School, Belfast, where a single room held 125 pupils.
(Hogg Collection, Ulster Museum)

Schools other than National schools had their own textbooks and one such is the *Historical Class-Book* by the Christian Brothers published in Dublin in 1860. Its contents include the Creation and the Deluge and outlines of Ancient, Modern, English and Irish history. In the chapter on Daniel O'Connell we read:

> On 13th of April 1829, by this peaceful revolution, in which "words were more than bottles", the Catholics of Great Britain were, with a few reservations, admitted to an equality of civil rights and privileges with their Protestant fellow-countrymen.

This concept of Catholic and Protestant fellow-countrymen, living in the island of Ireland in which Dublin was the capital and education was important and very similar, is pictorially demonstrated in the following photograph of the signwriting class in the College of Technology in the centre of Belfast in 1910.

It is important to notice the motto above the blackboard which is
'A NATION'S GREATNESS DEPENDS ON THE
EDUCATION OF ITS PEOPLE.'
(Hogg Collection, Ulster Museum)

The nation referred to is an undivided Ireland and is therefore the Irish nation. This is emphasised by the Irish greeting 'Cead Mile Failte' in a prominent position on the blackboard below the motto. Furthermore, the designs on the left and the right of the board are Celtic ones and would have been produced in 1910 by students at the signwriting class.

While there may not have been ill-will towards schools of other denominations, and the people of Ireland may have seen themselves as one nation living in four great provinces, there was controversy about the teaching of history in schools. On 1 September 1916 a letter from R. Kyle Knox of Belfast, was published in the *Belfast News Letter*. He stated:

> Boys are taught history in the schools in such a fashion as inculcates animosity and hatred against England, and incidentally against their fellow citizens. History has been made first a religious subject, and then a political machine. What can be expected from such teaching but senseless outbreaks like the Sinn Fein rebellion of 1916.

A memorandum about the teaching of history must have gone to National schools at this time and an even stronger attack was printed in the correspondence column of the same newspaper on 5 September. It is anonymously signed by A.C.O.B.

SEDITION IN NATIONAL SCHOOLS TO THE EDITOR OF THE BELFAST NEWSLETTER

> SIR, No notice need be taken of the "National" Education Board's memorandum re seditious training in "national" schools. It is simply the case for the defence as the Commissioners are the real respondents in the action. Until the exposure of the seditious "national reader", seditious readers and text books were sanctioned without any ceremony. There was a short lull in the storm on that occasion, but it was followed by a recrudescence of producing and sanctioning Anglophobian books. The Board gave extra vacations on the occasion of a) the Jubilee of Queen Victoria, b) her Diamond Jubilee, c) the Coronation of Edward VII, and d) the Coronation of George V. To insult their Sovereign in three-fourths of the "national" schools the priest managers ordered their State paid teachers to keep their schools open on these auspicious occasions, and to give the extra holidays at another time. The cowardly Commissioners acquiesced in this insulting and seditious policy. How could loyal citizens be

> produced in schools when disloyal "history" manuals are read, and disloyal "history" lessons are given, and where the Sovereign is openly insulted? Then again, were the State-paid teacher of a priest-ruled "national" school to give a loyal Empire lesson on Empire Day his priest-manager would give him a three months' notice, the "bishop" would countersign it, and neither the Government nor the National Education Board would move a little finger to save him from ruin. Does not anyone see that what is needed is the establishment of a Ministerial Department of Education, and the eviction of the priests from the schools, if they are not to continue to be in the future what they have been in the past - nurseries of sedition?

An examination of some of the textbooks in use in the period does not confirm this claim of 'seditious' textbooks. Both English and Irish history are presented objectively to the extent that in *A Short History of Ireland*, published in 1909 in Dublin, King William of Orange is described as 'one of the best generals of the time'. The Christian Brothers textbook, when describing the Anglo-Norman invasions, could hardly be accused of doing so in a seditious fashion.

> The condition of Ireland at the restoration was very peculiar. The rightful owners of the soil and the new adventurers viewed each other with a jealous eye. (1860)

This is not the type of language which would lead to insurgence and would not be considered seditious to us today. However, it is clear from the preceding letters that the teaching of history was a divisive issue in the decade before partition and was perhaps symbolic of the change in attitudes which were to come. In all other subjects the textbooks show that children in Ireland were provided with a very similar curriculum.

If this is so, then it should be remembered by Ena O'Neill, Norman Douglas, Annie Duff, Johnny Marquis, Mary Heatherington, John Parkinson and Teresa McCallam who were there.

CHAPTER SIX
SCHOOLDAYS REMEMBERED

Ena, Norman, Annie, Johnny, Mary, John and Teresa received no lessons from anyone before starting school and, except for John, all began school before the age of six. Ena went to a small National School in Leeson Street which was near her grandmother's home and Norman went to Cregagh Street National School, also in Belfast. Annie attended Bread Street National School which was just behind the ropeworks in east Belfast. She recalls a great fire which occurred in the ropeworks and trapped the children in their school where the teachers had to give them biscuits 'to keep the hunger off us'. They had already eaten the newspaper-wrapped lunches which they had brought to school and on which their names had been written by the teacher. When she began school in 1909,Annie begged her mother not to tell them that she was called Anne Jane in case she was ridiculed as 'My Aunt Jane'. ['My Aunt Jane' was a popular children's song at the time.] Consequently she became known as Jinny throughout her schooldays.

Johnny was only four when he started Cushendall National School in County Antrim and he has a hazy recollection of being hit for crying. He vividly recalls being at school during the coronation of George V in 1910 when they were all given medals and there were free rides on the hobby horses. At the age of four Mary started a church school in Church Road in Holywood. Her family then moved to Belfast and she went to Belmont School which is still in use.

John thinks that he was about six when he went to St. Philip's National school in Excise Street. His entry into school may have been delayed by the only illness he had as a child. 'It was just before I went to school, I was about five and I had diphtheria, which was very dangerous. I remember being carried out by the nurse to this special blackened ambulance and being taken to the fever hospital at Purdysburn. The ambulance was a big dark green coloured thing, like a police black maria, and it was specially fumigated. I can smell it yet. I was in the hospital for about six weeks and I well recall coming home. We came down from Purdysburn to the tramline in a wee pony and trap. There were no buses or taxis then and we had to travel the rest of the way home on the tram.'

Teresa went to St. Patrick's National school: 'I was at school very early, between three and four. I suppose they wanted rid of me. We were lucky because all we had to do was go over the hill, up the brae and down past the chapel. There were others had to walk three or four miles.'

There was no uniform at any of the National schools and all recollect children wearing frocks or skirts and jumpers, and short trousers. Both Johnny and John wore a uniform at Ballymena Academy and the Belfast Model and they had caps with the schools' initials on. Ena tells of one little boy still wearing petticoats when he came to school and she remembers it vividly because one day he wet himself and the teacher had to clean it up 'just like a skivvy'. Ena is still shocked at the idea of a teacher doing the work of a menial servant. Teresa laughs when she thinks of how they dressed: 'You wore ordinary clothes, no haute couture then. When you look at old school photographs it's awful: you've this dress hanging down and you're the same shape from top to bottom.'

Norman says that no child came to school without shoes, but Ena says that 'tons of them' were barefoot at her school and she remembers it well because they were put up the front near the fire to warm their feet and she was quite jealous of them getting so close to the fire. Annie's memory of this is very similar and she recalls a big fire with a fireguard around it at which bare-footed children were seated. She adds that when the watercart came round they all took their shoes off for the 'fun of it' and chased after the cart. [A watercart was a horse-drawn cart that came around the streets and sprayed water on the ground to keep the dust down.] Johnny remembers some children without shoes, but says that there were only a few and they were the extreme cases of poverty. No children were without shoes at Mary's school but she says that poorer children went to a church school at Strandtown and some of them were barefoot. Some children at John's school wore light shoes, called mutton dummies, in the summertime: 'I tell you what we did wear in the primary school: we wore clogs. They had leather tops and wooden soles the same as you would buy in Holland. We used to come home for lunch and my mother would know to have the soup poured out because she heard us running up the street with our clogs on. I don't remember anyone barefoot in the winter. My sister would wear button boots, buttoned right up to the knee.'

Teresa is quite sure on the question of shoes: 'I don't remember any without them. I wasn't allowed to go out in bare feet and I would have loved it. I used to see these big fellows coming down the brae in the warm weather and there might have been blood coming out of their toes where they'd hit them. They seemed to enjoy it. I don't think anybody was in bare feet because they were too poor to buy shoes. We used to sit along the wall at playtime and look at each other's shoes. One girl was a bit soft in the head and she used to shuffle along and ruin her shoes and we used to say to her "another new pair of shoes". We were dying to get so many shoes. Hers was a case of having to. Even the country ones had shoes.'

Coming to school without shoes does not seem to have been as widespread as Ena and Annie imagine, though Johnny and Mary recall a few cases. In chatting to others who were at school at the time only two other people could recollect children coming barefooted and they were a lady who began St.Aidan's School, Belfast in 1916 who said that some children came without shoes because they were poor, and a gentleman who started the Presbyterian Church School in Downpatrick in 1915 who said that some came without shoes but there were 'very few such'. No one else recalled any children without shoes, including ones who started school on the Shankill Road in 1911, Rostrevor National School in 1913, Finiston National School in Belfast in 1909, Antrim Road Baptist Church School in 1907, St. Saviour's School in 1915 , Duncairn Methodist Church Hall in 1916, and Old Bedford Infants' School in Belfast in 1913.

One gentleman was so incensed when I suggested that maybe he just did not remember those without shoes that he brought me a photograph of the entire enrolment of Madrid Street National School, taken in 1918, and indeed not one child, including himself, is barefooted.

Madrid Street National School, Belfast, 1918
(Courtesy of Robert Morrow)

Everyone remembers progression through school as passing from infants to senior infants, then first class, second class through until sixth class, the last. All recall people not passing into the next class. Annie describes the process as 'going through books one to six and when you finished book six you could leave'.This was a process she did not complete: 'I wasn't very smart at school. I didn't finish the book, but I remember a young boy called Kerr, he was very clever and he went through the books quickly. He left before he was fourteen and ended up as a manager in the shipyard. Wasn't that great?' Annie is still filled with admiration for this accomplishment of Kerr's, especially because 'he was small and he never grew very tall but he did well.'

According to Norman, there was no passing or failing in infants, but from class one you had to pass an exam to get into class two, 'it wasn't an automatic switch around.' This exam would most likely have been based on the National reading books, 'readers', in use at the time and Norman recalls that you were most likely to be held back up to fourth class. Ena remembers that two or three girls were kept back and politely says that it was because 'the class was too advanced for them'. Johnny recounts the progression as going through standards when you were supposed to reach standard seven by the age of thirteen. Mary confirms this and even names her teachers: 'We passed through the classes if we were able. Miss Ogle had Babies and Senior Infants, Miss Ross taught first, second and third class and she was a cheeky old thing. Miss Ogle was a nicer teacher and she lived about the Ravenhill Road. I reached the higher grades and did a big exam. I was the only one to get honours. We had to go Mountpottinger School that Saturday morning to sit the examination, there were three of us that went together. We travelled down on the tram and one of them brought her books to look at on the way down. She failed it! I was the only one passed and I was delighted when they called out "Mary Heatherington, Honours".'

John reached standard seven by the age of twelve, so was able to sit the examination for the Belfast Model which was a much sought after school for pupils from all over the city. The headmaster was a man called Waxy Haslett: 'He was called this because he had a wax moustache. He always had two canes down the side of his legs, a long one and a short one. He used the cane according to the crime, a bad crime got the long cane and a not so bad crime got the short one. Corporal punishment was the done thing in those days.'

There was corporal punishment in Teresa's school too: 'I don't remember ever getting slapped by the teachers at school, but plenty of slapping went on. Mrs. Larmour, that was one of our teachers, she used to bring me up if I did something and say, "Now, now, Teresa, we'll never make a lady out of you." I did get slapped by the other children, and punched. I couldn't help being able to do the things and I was always singled out. I really just wanted to be like everyone else. I can understand youngsters now when they talk about this bullying, for it really is something you don't want.'

Teresa's school had four rooms: 'The school was divided in two and one half was for the boys and the other half was for the girls. In each half there were two rooms: a great big room and a small room no bigger than a living room. There was a big coal fire and that heated both rooms, if you were at the back you were freezing. And you couldn't see out of the windows so there were no distractions. You moved from one standard to the next but that just meant moving around the big room.'

When asked what subjects they were taught at school, the responses were initially very similar.

Ena: Tables and subtraction and division. Handwriting was very important, one line on top and you had to copy it, like copperplate, every day.

Norman: Writing, reading, spelling, arithmetic, geography. On a slate in the early days. Then we got a book with beautiful copperplate writing, things like I like going to school and we'd to copy below that twice and that was done from the very early stages. It was a very important subject, maybe about half an hour each day. Spelling was another important subject.

Annie: We did a lot of sums, short dividing and long dividing and multiplication. We used a slate when we were very young and when we got bigger, we got a jotter. We had to do writing every single day and I hated that. I wasn't very good at it.

Johnny: We did a lot of English, reading and writing on a slate. There was lots of parsing. We used *Sullivan's Grammar* and I was very good at it. [Johnny proceeded to give me a lesson on tenses and past participles and without hesitation recited all the prepositions and conjunctions.] Maths was important too and we did algebra and geometry as well as ordinary maths. I could do equations before I left National school. We did history and geography and there was a great emphasis on handwriting and neatness.

Mary: We did arithmetic, English, geography, drawing and composition. We had to learn things off by heart and you learned them so well I can still remember one of the poems from Belmont National School eighty years ago:

A primrose awoke from its long winter sleep
And stretched out its head through the green leaves to peep,
But the air was so cold and the wind was so keen

Not a bright flower but itself could be seen.
Alas, said the primrose, no use to deny
Here all alone half-hidden I lie.
I'll try to be cheerful, contented to be
Just a simple wild flower growing under a tree.
Soon a maiden passed by looking weary and sad,
In the bright Irish springtime when all should be glad.
She saw the primrose so bright and so gay,
And decided it charmed all her sadness away.
The primrose gave thanks to the dear Lord above
Who had sent along such a submission of love.

Ever since that I've loved primroses but it makes me sad to think of the wee primrose on its own. We also did a lot of handwriting, in copybooks with one line written and six lines to copy on.

John: We concentrated on the famous three Rs - reading, writing and 'rithmetic. We were also taught geography. In the National school we followed set books. A man called Hugh Campbell was the headmaster. In the Belfast Model we did all the subjects and had a different teacher for each one.

Teresa: English, maths, geography, a bit of history and a lot of writing. Oh the handwriting was great: the Vere Foster copybook with the headline and four lines for your writing. You had to keep your writing uniform. But you didn't start off with that, we started with a queer kind of thing. It wasn't a slate; it was more like hardboard; it was longer than it was wide and you got chalk to do your work on it, first of all as you sat at the big long desk. In writing you went from the straight lines to the curves, and the qs and the slanted lines and then to joined writing. Then you went to the Headline copybooks, you'd to write half a page of maybe 'Roses are red, violets are blue'. You had to cross your fs just on this line; it had to be right. And then the pens, maybe the tip was twisted and the ink went scooting and there was a blot and that was another row. It was hard work, very laborious.

Handwriting was obviously an important part of the curriculum when it is remembered vividly by all. That this was stressed and was indeed copperplate can be seen from the following examples of handwriting from some of those who were at school at this time.

Comments about your schooldays. ....Very happy.....
...We worked hard & competed for
..prizes at end of each Term.........

Grace Kennedy D.O.B. 23 April 1902

Comments about your schooldays. ...Mixed class, with childhood romances
.....long summer holidays.....getting caned for something I did
....not do..........................

William McMordie D.O.B. 29 June 1903

There was 'Curfew' and the penalty of breaking that was certain death,
I was at an age when I was home early anyway & it didn't affect me really, but I was very aware of it.

Ena McKenna D.O.B. 17 February 1905

So we find lack of trust forms a good part of our lives as individuals, as a nation and indeed of the World.

Norman Douglas D.O.B. 28 December 1909

That Ena does not immediately recall geography as one of her school subjects may be due to the fact that she was very bad at it when in school and got into trouble for her failure to learn it. When asked about geography while discussing individual subjects, she said: 'I was very bad at that. We did it all like rhymes, so you would remember it but I was no good at learning them.'

Norman's response confirms the idea of learning in metre but it is obvious that he was somewhat better at the subject: 'It was all Irish geography. You did it in rhyme form, for example From Fair Head in Antrim to Mizen Head in Cork, that's how you learned the most northerly and southerly points of the country. And the rivers - Dublin's on the Liffey, Cork's on the Lee. And the counties - Queen's County, King's County, Wicklow, etcetera.'

Annie remembers learning many of the capitals in the world and Johnny presents a broader geography curriculum which is the same as the textbooks. He was also able to complete the second line for Norman.

Johnny: We did plenty of geography. We started with the world, then the British Empire and then Ireland. To this day I know every shire in England and every river, mountain, headland and inlet in Ireland. We learned them like a recitation:

From Fair Head in Antrim
To Mizen Head in Cork,
From Howth Head in Dublin
To Slyne head in Galway.

Mary enjoyed the subject: 'I liked geography and we did a lot of it, it was good about the different countries. Even now if my son mentions Athy, I say Naas, Athy, Kildare, Maynooth. They were four of the towns in Kildare, we learnt it all in rhyme. And if I hear a district in England I can rhyme them off too; we were given three at a time to learn all the way down England.'

Being asked about geography elicited a flood of memories from Teresa: 'We did geography all right and we had great big maps on rollers on the wall. One day I was asked to point out Argentina. I knew it was yellow but dear me, could I find it on the map? I just waved the pointer and said it's about here somewhere and the teacher was very sarcastic and threw a book at me. You see, usually I got it right. The inspector came down every year and I hated it; it wasn't because I didn't like him but I was always brought out to answer the questions. It was like going in for an operation. I was the only wee'n that was brought out and I didn't think I was any different. The teacher that we had was Mrs Larmour, the second assistant. I don't know what her qualifications were, but her husband died and she suddenly started teaching. She taught us about Ireland and we knew nothing. One day the first assistant took us and she went round the map of Ireland.

What a disgrace, we knew nothing. She asked us the towns of each county but we didn't know them. I was lucky because I got Down and I was able to give her Downpatrick because it was only six miles away. She was absolutely disgusted and said we knew more about foreign countries. We'd to learn it all again. When I told my mother she said some teachers just made their way through and she could remember one year when my father was the only one who got result fees for the proficiency of his class. In his day teachers got extra pay if their pupils did well, it was like a reward for good teachers. They all said my father was a great teacher and his staff thought the world of him. People told me that years after he died they could still remember the things he had taught them. I wish I'd more than a photograph to remember him by.'

Teresa's father, extreme left, on a school staff outing
before she was born.

Ena, Annie and Mary do not remember any science being taught and Norman and Johnny recall it only in fifth and sixth class. John did science only when he attended the post-national school. Johnny says that they had a balance and weighed things and did some experiments on the stove in the national school. The only science Teresa ever did was to make soap out of potatoes and they had to 'shake and shake for eternity' until they got bubbles. Science in school was obligatory from 1920, but it was not often available owing to lack of funds. Norman and Johnny were perhaps fortunate to get any science in National school.

When asked about religion, Ena remembers only learning the catechism at school while Norman says that they had a reading from the Bible, a verse of scripture and a prayer each morning. Neither recalls any form of assembly or hymn-singing. Annie and Johnny both started their school days with a prayer, but do not think that religion had any special emphasis in their schools. Mary's school was connected to the Presbyterian church, so religion was taught each morning. Surprisingly all the children did not have their lessons in religion together, one teacher taught the Church of Ireland pupils and the another teacher took the Presbyterian ones. John enjoyed the religion he learned at school and vividly remembers the minister coming in each year. He still has the certificates which he was awarded at these annual inspections.

Teresa had lessons in religion each morning and a canon came up to the school to ask them questions. Her memories are not always of the religious aspect of these visits: 'We had a shock one day when the Canon came in. The teacher sat at a desk at the top and alongside her were the pupils' long desks, only they were lower. Between the long desk and hers it made a sort of shelf, so she had all her books there with an elastic round them to keep them in place. It was very handy for her to reach them without getting up. This day the canon pulled the elastic back and made it pop. "What's this," he says, "garters?" We all giggled because we couldn't believe he'd said such a thing.'

Norman does not have any recollection of history being taught, which is surprising when his recall of the geography is so good. Annie says that 'it wasn't bothered with' in her school. Not much history was taught in Mary's school which pleased her because she didn't like the subject. John studied history only in the Belfast Model. Ena, Johnny and Teresa do remember learning history.

Ena: We were taught history but it wasn't like the history taught nowadays. We did Irish history, all about Brian Boru and the big giants like Cuchulain and Finn MacCool.

Johnny: We did British history and got quite a dose of Irish history too. I can still recite Poynings Law and I can remember every detail of the siege of Derry. There was a picture on the wall of every king from William the Conqueror to George V.

Teresa: I hated history. The book had small print and it was made of cheap paper. All those lists of kings, Henry this and Henry that and a bit of Irish history.

Perhaps this is a reflection of the debate which was raging regarding the teaching of history, and Norman's, Annie's, Mary's and John's National schools simply did not teach any since it wasn't obligatory. History textbooks of the period offered British and Irish history, so it is interesting that in mainly Protestant schools neither was taught. It is equally interesting that Ena remembers only being taught Irish history before the Plantation, and Johnny and Teresa's teachers dwelt so much on British monarchs.

When asked about whether or not their parents encouraged them to do homework, the attitudes and aspirations are very similar:

Ena: They didn't have to. You see the teachers were freer to make you then. They would just have slapped the hands off you and you wouldn't have told. You thought they were God Almighty. You wouldn't have gone in without your work done.

Norman: They did. You had to do the right thing if you were to save yourself from punishment in school. I couldn't play until it was done. If your work in school was untidy, you were sent to the corner for the next half hour. The headmaster came round on the half hour and you got two across your hand with the cane. I found this very strange because the same man who caned me got me to come round to his house to play the piano for meetings at night.

Annie: My mother always told me to get my homework done because I would get slapped in school if I didn't. I got slapped anyway because I was never very good at school.

Johnny: My mother believed that the only way we could make something of ourselves was to get educated. I was good at school but my elder sister was a dope and I had to help her with her homework as well. After I finished at the National School, I was at home and a man came and asked if I could take a job delivering. My mother chased him and said that I was too smart to be a delivery boy. There was no Catholic grammar school so she went to see the headmaster of Ballymena Academy, a Protestant school, she was that determined I would finish my education. The headmaster said that he didn't care what religion I was as long as I was clever and worked, so he gave me a test. I was admitted and spent the next two years there. My mother encouraged me all the way.

Mary: You were always expected just to go to school and you were never kept off for anything. My mother always worked with me at home because I was very good at figures and she wanted me to do well in school.

John: My parents always encouraged me to work at school and do my homework. There wasn't much homework at the National school but there was plenty at the Model. They didn't want me to leave school.

Teresa: My mother really wanted me to have plenty of schooling and, even after I'd finished, she sent me down to the technical for commercial subjects. I didn't want to go, but when your mother said you went, you went.

When asked 'When you went to school, what country did you think you lived in?' Ena replied without hesitation 'Ireland'. Norman's response was rather more hesitant: 'I don't think I cared what country I lived in. Had to be Ireland, but we didn't think much about it. Having been taught the geography, that was my natural reaction. I was Irish.' Annie said that she lived in Belfast in Ireland when she was young, but it was never really talked about. Johnny's reply was more voluble.

Johnny: I knew that I lived in Ireland but there was no anti-British hassle. I was more interested in the World War. Catholics supported the army. A board outside the newsagent's in Ballymena had notices about the war and I remember reading them. The telegram messengers went by bike and after the Somme I remember Catholic and Protestant families receiving telegrams. That was a terrible sad day. The Waveney hospital was built for the recuperation of soldiers; they wore blue uniforms and often came into the cafe. Then they were moved on to Shane's castle in Antrim. My mother had no time for bigotry of any description. She often said that I was reared on Protestant money since her clients were Orangemen from the Braid [a Protestant area of Ballymena].

Mary repeated the question in a tone of voice that implied only an idiot would ask such a simple question and then answered: 'Ireland. It was only one country.' John was silent for a long time. ''We were always very Protestant and very British, yet we did live in Ireland then.' Teresa answered immediately 'Ireland'.

Ena had no idea what her parents thought about the name of the country they lived in since 'it never came into it; England was away out of the world.' Norman thought that his parents would have viewed their country as Ireland: 'You see, there was never any talk of partition. It was a world war that we were fighting then and we had volunteers from Ireland, regiments from Ireland, the Inniskilling Fusiliers, the Royal Irish Fusiliers, the Munster Hussars and all those sort of things in those days. When I started school, the thrust must have been to win the war against the Germans. There was no question of partition.'

The question of what the capital was when she started school rather stumped Ena who, I think, thought it was a trick question. She replied that she had never thought about it and that it was never talked about then. 'All we really cared about were the people who lived round us and in our city. Any big event affected us all. I can recall when the word came through that the *Titanic* had gone down and I was taken to light a candle to pray for all the people on board. There were candles in many of the windows in our street that night. We cared more because Belfast men had built that ship. Dublin was too far away to think about.

Norman and John replied, slightly begrudgingly, to the same question: 'It must have been Dublin'. Annie had never heard the matter discussed, but Johnny replied immediately: 'Dublin was the capital. Belfast was the provincial capital, a big city that I went to for the first time in 1914 to get glasses in Glenravel Street. My aunt was married to Captain Morgan of the Royal Irish Rifles and he met us in Belfast and took us to Victoria Barracks. This was a huge place where soldiers could be garrisoned in times of emergency. Mostly the men were single but there were quarters for some married soldiers.'

Mary pondered for a moment: 'Was it London or Dublin? I never really thought about it then. It must have been Dublin. My brother, who was born in 1907, qualified in Dublin, he has M.P.S. (Member of the Pharmaceutical Society) after his name, and yet now it's M.P.S. N.I.(Northern Ireland), you see it in all the chemist shops. He didn't need the N.I.'

Teresa said that she never thought about it either at the time but according to their schoolbooks it must have been Dublin. She knew that it wasn't Belfast, it was just the provincial capital.

Playing churchie, a robust kind of leap-frog, was of more interest to schoolchildren at the start of the century.
(Hogg Collection, Ulster Museum)

CHAPTER SEVEN
LEISURE TIME REMEMBERED

All young children played in the street each day after they had finished their homework. According to Johnny they played games which 'all had their season' [i.e. were popular according to the weather or time of year]. They would have played with anyone who lived nearby and had no objections to playing with the opposite sex. Ena played skipping, hopscotch and round the world, while Norman remembers playing football, rounders, marbles which were known as marlies, and 'something of the nature of hopscotch.' Annie enjoyed skipping and piggy and 'bulked the marlies' when she played with them. She explained that in games with marbles 'bulking' was a method of hitting them while 'funkyknuckle' was not being able to fire them with a straight forefinger.

Johnny played marbles too, as well as chestnuts, pirries [wooden tops with string that you wrapped around your finger and released to make the pirrie move], churchie-one-over and hiking across the bay. He thought that a bicycle was everything and he once went from Ballymena to Belfast on his bicycle. Mary liked to play wee shops and Farmer's Wife type of games. John played football in the street or the park and he enjoyed swimming: 'We went swimming after school to the Ormeau Baths. The headmaster gave you a wee note and if there were at least six of you, you got in for half price.' He also played with chestnuts and they reminded him of his milkman. 'He came round with milk straight from the fields, it wasn't pasteurised or anything. He used to bring us chestnuts in autumn and sometimes he even took us out in his cart to the country to collect the chestnuts.' Teresa didn't like playing hoops and she used to get into trouble when she played marbles because she ran home with them and the wee boys chased her.

Many homes had musical instruments for evening entertainment. In Ena's home there was a piano and in Norman's there was a harmonium. One of Mary's brothers had a violin and another one played a sixpenny mouthorgan which he had got for Christmas. John's brother played a mandolin and because his sister was very musical his father bought her a lovely piano. Teresa's family always enjoyed music: 'There were plenty of musical instruments about the house, bagpipes and brass band instruments. Gerard was in the brass band and he played a great big thing called a bombardon. I had the job of cleaning that brass thing every week for him going down to the band practice, it was a day's work. And then there was pipe band as well and two brothers were in that.' There wasn't the money for instruments in Annie's home but she treasured pieces of broken delph that she collected, polished and used to play houses.

Is anyone 'bulking the marlies' in this early twentieth-century scene?
(Hogg Collection, Ulster Museum)

John was the only one to follow a particular team: 'Distillery Football Club, that was the team that I supported because they were on our street. They had mixed players, Roman Catholic and Protestant. The religion of teams depended on the area the players came from, or the factory or mill the team was connected with. In those days Linfield wouldn't have had a Roman Catholic player, it was attached to the Linfield Mill in Sandy Row. The name came from the linen fields. Distillery was a mixed club, that was another reason why we supported it.' Norman and Johnny watched local cricket and football teams, but didn't really follow one. Mary's brothers were football fans, one of Linfield and another of Glentoran.

John was a member of the Boys' Brigade and Norman was in the Scouts. He chuckles as he recounts his experiences at camp:

'When I was a boy I went with the nineteenth Scouts to camp in Donaghadee. We slept in bell tents, four to a tent, no sleeping bags then; we slept on a ground sheet with a blanket over us. The four leaders had their own tent and the cook, a Scotsman called Anderson, slept in his own tent beside his alarm clock. He got up at half past six to make breakfast before reveille at seven thirty.

One night the boys in my tent decided to paint all the others with Cherry Blossom shoe polish. We stayed awake until they had all gone asleep. I had the polish and a fellow called Dunwoody held the candle, he was too fat to creep into the tents. We painted faces on all the boys and on one fellow whose pyjamas were open I painted the word OXO on his stomach. We did the leaders too and on the skipper Frank O'Neill's face I put a big Kung Foo moustache. When we did Anderson, the cook, he stirred in his sleep and half sat up. We got away and he fell back to sleep but as he did he fell on his alarm clock and knocked it over. We went back to our tent, did our own faces, wiped our hands on the grass and went to sleep.

There was an unholy row in the morning. The glass on Anderson's clock had broken and the wet from the grass had got into it and stopped it so he hadn't wakened up. When we were all assembled O'Neill shouted at us to try to find out who had done it. Nobody would own up and every time we looked at the moustache on his face we all laughed. He found it hard to keep a straight face every time he looked at the twenty of us. He threatened to send us all home but he didn't. Anderson was the angriest of all.'

Mary belonged to the Girls' Friendly, an organisation in St. Mark's church which a lady called Miss Brown ran, and there she made raffia things for sales of work. Her mother wasn't very keen on such organisations: 'I was the youngest person in the church choir and that was all right, even though the minister's wife was so snooty she wouldn't let her own children come to the Sunday school. My mother disapproved of some organisations. Once my brother joined the Church Lads' Brigade but she thought it was too much like the army and wouldn't let him go back. He didn't get to be in it for more than the one night.' Teresa was a member of many church organisations, Sodality, Imelda Society and Handmaidens, and also played tennis and badminton.

Norman had three cats and Ena's father bred Airedales. Her family also had whippets - which won money, two ponies called Susannah and Graball, and a pony for the trap. Johnny's family kept bantams which ended up in the pot at the cafe when their laying days were over. Mary always had a dog but her parents weren't keen on cats. John was only allowed a cat and Teresa had a cat as well as a dog.

When asked whether anyone ever went to concerts, cinemas or music halls, the following answers were given.

Ena: Oh, yes. I went to the Alhambra in Lower North Street, and the Gaiety, and the Clonard Picture House, and Johnny Donnelly's in Albert Street, and there was the Coliseum and the Hippodrome. I once went to see Harry Lauder.

Norman: The Grosvenor Hall ran cinema shows. The first time I was in a cinema was with a Roman Catholic called Winnie Loughran and she took me to the Willowfield to see Charlie Chaplin. I can still see Winnie, a big dark girl. They were a lovely family, the Loughrans; they were very great friends; they used to come in, knock the back door, come in by the back door and have a yarn with my mother. It was in 1920 that I first went to the pictures.

This reply reveals a great deal more than information about cinemas. Norman is keen to stress his and his family's lack of bigotry, his own by referring to the Loughrans as a lovely family and his family's by the fact that the Loughrans came into their home by the back door. Friends always used the back door because it led into the heart of the home, the kitchen, while strangers were brought in by the front door - to the impersonal and rarely used parlour. It may also reveal the differing attitudes at the time regarding picture houses and the fact that it was a Catholic who first took Norman to one may indicate that he considered Catholic attitudes to be more liberal. This is further emphasised later when he is discussing entertainment: 'There were cinemas in those days, but the family I was brought up in didn't know much about cinemas. Well, possibly Bertie did. I had to go to church so cinemas didn't come into your way of life.'

When talking about his older brother Bertie, Norman produced a photograph which he remembered having taken with his brother before Bertie went off to war in 1914. He thinks that he went for training first to Finner Camp, Bundoran, Co. Donegal with the 36th Ulster Division. He is now surprised that this should have been so, though he says that he saw nothing unusual in the choice of training camp at the time. Bertie was Norman's eldest brother [who fought in World War I], so possibly he was viewed as a man of the world and therefore it was permissible for him to go to cinemas.

Norman and Bertie
1914

That Annie stopped going to the cinema after she was 'saved' reinforces the fact that some Protestants thought that going to the pictures was a sin. Annie's first response to whether or not she went to cinemas was quite different: 'Oh yes, lots. To the Old Princess and the New Princess. I can still remember watching Pearl Buck and Andy Reed the cowboy.'

Johnny went to a range of events and even benefited from his academic ability: 'We went to the cinema once a week, every Saturday. They were all silent films like Charlie Chaplin. I read to a bad reader for some sweets. [In silent films the captions came up on the screen and a child unable to read would have had difficulty following the plot.] Children in those days were great at sharing! There was one hall in the town and my mother took us to plays there when touring companies came. I can remember going to see *H.M.S. Pinafore, The Pirates of Penzance and The Worst Woman in London.* Gilbert and Sullivan wrote the first two but I can't remember the author of the last one. It was a Protestant hall but, as I've told you, everyone mixed. No one cared what religion you were, we all went to the same hall. Then in 1916 or 1917 they built a Catholic hall in Broughshane Street. I played billiards there when I was underage, that's how I know when it was built. At the time I didn't think of the halls as being Catholic or Protesant.'

Mary: We never got going to the pictures. My mother didn't think it was good for us and we would get carried away with romantic ideas.

John's reply shows that going to the cinema was not denied to church-going families: 'The cinema was a part of our life. There was a cinema called the Coliseum on the corner of Sandy Row. We went there to matinees on a Saturday, a penny or tuppence to get in.'

Teresa: You wouldn't have missed a concert for the world. There was no cinema in Portaferry but I went to the Empire in Belfast when we went up to see my sister, Brigid, who worked in Belfast.

The differing attitude to entertainment is borne out by the recollections of everyone as to whether or not their parents went to music halls or cinemas. No real religious difference is shown. Norman has no memory of his parents ever going to such places, even though his mother was very musical and loved to go into the parlour and play the harmonium.

Ena, however, has vivid memories: 'Certainly, they went to music halls and cinemas and they never missed the ballet. Of course it was just being introduced to Belfast then and it was very crude. There was a lot of talk at home once about a great play which my father went to see in the Opera House. It was all about Napoleon divorcing Josephine and some people thought it wasn't respectable because it was about divorce. I remember my father making us laugh by telling how people pelted Napoleon with tomatoes.'

The audience at the Grand Opera House, Saturday 4 August 1917.
(Hogg Collection, Ulster Museum)

The performance was the last night of A Royal Divorce, a popular tale of Napoleon and Josephine. Incidental music was provided by the band of the Royal Irish Constabulary. This photograph, taken by Alex Hogg, confirms this memory of Ena's. Her information about some people not thinking it respectable, because divorce was the subject matter, may explain why some people were hiding their faces. The note, by the social historian, W.A. Maguire, which accompanies the photograph, indicates that he did not know why faces were being hidden.

Annie's parents were also picture-goers. 'My parents didn't have much money to spare but if they had some they loved to go to the pictures. They used to follow up a picture for several weeks and my father would tell us how each night ended. Once it ended with great wooden gates and a man holding them closed with his body because wild lions were trying to get in. My parents had to go back to find out the upshot.'

Johnny's mother was much too busy to go out often. 'My mother never had much spare time, she worked so hard but she took us to plays if she could. Just occasionally she would go to a ceile house in the country with all the other women. There they sat in the good room and drank punch - hot water, sugar and whiskey. Of course she never went into a public house; only women of ill-repute went there.'

Mary's parents did not go out much: her father was busy with earning enough to keep his family and her mother with looking after the five children. There was not much time for entertainment for John's parents either because his father worked a great deal of overtime, especially when they were building the *Titanic*: 'He used to work fifty-four hours a week - that was his ordinary working week - and then he worked overtime. He went out at half past six every morning.' Teresa's mother never went to ceiles but she loved concerts, the pipes and singing.

While Ena was at school, her Saturdays were spent helping her father by delivering things. Sometimes she was given a penny to go to the matinee. Norman went to the park and watched cricket if it was a good day, or else he went to watch football. Two of the teams he remembers well in the league which he watched were Sandown and Mount Avon, teams that no longer exist.

Before going out to play on a Saturday Norman had to help with chores around the house. His most hated job was when he had to take the brass stair-rods off the lino on the stairs and bring them down and polish them. Sometimes he even got up to mischief in his leisure time: 'You see, there was no vandalism then; anything we did was more devilment. Mr. Campbell up at the corner used to have a shop, cigarettes and confectionery. We used to write in the window, bacon, such and such a pound. Things he didn't keep, you know. We maybe left it up for an hour. Of course if my father knew I had done that he'd have hammered the life and soul out of me. But we left it up for an hour and then asked Mrs. Campbell for a duster and rubbed it off. There was no badness in me.'

Annie's Saturdays were taken up with helping her mother in the mornings, going to the shop or getting water from the watering cart. These chores done, she, like Ena, was free to go the matinee at the pictures in the afternoon.

Johnny helped around his mother's cafe on Saturday mornings and earned the pocket money which took him to the pictures.

One penny seems to have been the usual amount for a child to have received as pocket money, but it could go a long way. Norman could get two stomach cakes [large, flat, spicy biscuits] for a halfpenny from Co-op breadservers when they returned to the bakery in his street after their day's delivering and Annie's penny took her to pictures four times. Johnny was able to buy thirteen Riley's butternuts for a halfpenny, but he was fortunate in that he had the opportunity to earn extra money.

Johnny: I helped in the cafe on Saturdays and I got a bit extra from some customers, especially on cattle show days. They were big days in Ballymena. I remember that my mother made fifty pounds in one day. That was a fortune then. If I got too much from customers, my mother took it off me to save.

DUNCAIRN ESTATE.

TWO SUPERIOR

TERRACE HOUSES,

MOYOLA STREET.

IN ONE LOT OR SINGLY.

To be Sold by Public AUCTION, at the AUCTION MART, 8 BERRY STREET, on FRIDAY, 25th October, 1918, at ONE o'clock.

THOSE TWO SUPERIOR TERRACE HOUSES, 41-43 MOYOLA STREET.

Let at £17 each		£34 0 0
Ground Rent £8 15 0 (adjusted)		
Less Collected out of No. 39	3 0 0—£5 15 0	
Taxes, say	6 10 0—12 5 0	
Profit Rental		£21 15 0

The Houses contain Parlour, 3 Bedrooms, etc. The situation is a most desirable one. Persons wishing to purchase a nice Terrace House as a Residence or as an Investment could not be better suited.

JAMES A. CULBERT, Solicitor,
11 Chichester Street.

ABRAHAM NEILL & CO.,
Auctioneers, 8 Berry Street.

DRUG BARGAINS No. 1.

NEW?—YES; BUT IN ORDER TO MAKE THE EARLY CLOSING

(At present 9 o'clock sharp)

MORE POPULAR, AND TO INDUCE PATRONS AT

BROWNE'S DRUG HALL,

381 WOODSTOCK ROAD,

TO MAKE THEIR PURCHASES AS EARLY AS POSSIBLE.

I AM OFFERING, EVERY DAY

During the Week

(WEDNESDAY EXCEPTED)

Till 5 p.m.

Parrish's Chemical Food,

In 6oz. Bottles at 10d, 8oz. 1s 1d Each.

After which hour the Usual Price of 1s 3d and 1s 6d will be charged.

J. BROWNE, Druggist,

381 WOODSTOCK ROAD.

Famous for Chesterfields

Ne r in our successful history was this more justified.

Settees, 3 piece and 7 piece Suites are now on show on our floors in elegant profusion—all boldly marked at prices that will astonish you.

Let us show you :—

The "Ruddleigh"	The "Fairholme"	The "Dene"	The "Raffield"
£11 15 0	£15 10 0	£18 5 0	£26 10 0

AMIDST A HOST OF OTHERS.

Fifty Sideboards Also.

YOUNG & COMPANY

40 High Street, - - - BELFAST

Fifty pounds was indeed a fortune then, especially to a small boy, and purchased a great deal.

(All advertisements from the *Belfast Telegraph*, 24 October 1918.)

There were few extras for Annie:
'If I was lucky, I got a penny on a Friday night when my daddy came home but we didn't have a lot of money. I remember once my mother sent me for sugar. She gave me a penny and the sugar was three farthings. The shopman said he didn't have any farthings and would I take sweets instead. I said yes but when I came home my mother said "where's the farthing?" I told her what had happened and she said "take the sweets back and get matches." They were poor days. Sometimes my mother had to send my father's suit to the pawn on Monday and get it back for him on Friday when my father or somebody came into money. She would say " run away over quickly and get the suit out of your uncle's." They didn't say the pawn. She might send you back with it the next Monday. They wouldn't take from children in the pawn, so you had to stand outside and wait for a woman and say "Missis are you going in, can I go in with you?" She'd put the parcel up for you. Our nearest pawn was on the corner of Witham Street. Them days were terrible when you'd no money.'

Mary had no regular pocket money:
'We didn't get pocket money, sometimes you were given something if your parents could afford it but you were well fed and all that. We never really wanted for anything, we got whatever was going. Maybe my mother got a wee bucket of apples, the man came round with a horse and cart and sold a bucket for sixpence. Kemps they called these apples and we were delighted because they were a lovely sweet Irish apple. Now and again we got sweets; my granny might have given us a penny. Sometimes I minded somebody's child on a Saturday and I might have got something for that.'

John was given 'a matter of pence only. If somebody gave you sixpence, you thought you were the King.' Teresa had no regular pocket money but she was sometimes given a penny or three farthings: 'Then I would buy sweets, black balls or clove rock. The sweets were kept in four-quart cans with lids and when they were empty they were sold for four pence. We used them to carry buttermilk from the farm. Sometimes the buttermilk wasn't any good and my mother used to call it green water. The woman on the farm, Margaret Ann, was very small and when she bent over the big churns with a ladle to get the buttermilk, I always thought she would fall in so I watched carefully. I went the messages for my mother on a Saturday and got everything in for the weekend. I remember one Saturday during the war when I was sent down for a loaf. There was a shortage of the brown paper that they used to wrap everything in and there was only a wee bit of paper round the loaf. The ends were open and the flour was very black. Hugh Savage and James McGratten used to stand at the gate where you came up from the town and when I passed Hugh Savage shouted "Ah-ha, that's not a very white loaf." I was so embarrassed that I was in a bad way and I never wanted to go for the rations again.'

Ena, Norman, Annie, Johnny, Mary, John and Teresa never missed Church on Sunday. Ena went with her parents or else with her grandmother if her parents were away. Norman had to accompany both his parents to the Baptist Tabernacle twice each Sunday. Other Church activities which he attended were Sunday School parties and Children's days when he sang with the children's choir. Ena took part in Devotions and Missions at Lent. Annie went to the East End Baptist Church morning and night and to Sunday School in the Iron Mission hall in the afternoons. Johnny attended church every Sunday with his mother and sisters and always arrived early as he was an acolyte and helped serve Mass. Mary and her brothers and sister were all sent to Sunday school in St. Mark's and then on to church. She enjoyed Sunday afternoons better because her parents took them all for walks up around Belmont. John's family were members of Christchurch in Durham Street and Teresa's family worshipped together and paid two pounds a year for the seat. This was a common practice in churches and reminded Norman of the time when he was a boy and his family visited a church in Ballynahinch: 'Our whole family went into the Presbyterian church there one Sunday morning and sat down in a pew about three from the back. A few minutes later a well-dressed gentleman and two ladies came in. They stopped at the end of the pew and just stood there glaring at us. They didn't speak but we realised that it was their pew. We had to get up in front of everybody and move to another seat. It was very embarrassing and my father would never go back to that church again.'

In the school summer holidays Norman went to stay with relations in Ballynahinch. His most enduring memory is of marble competitions in the

Diamond there because even grown men played. For holidays, Norman remembers only ever going with his mother because his father was away so much. Once they went to Islandmagee and on another occasion around 1916, which he recalls vividly, they went to Portavogie:

'We got the tramcar down to Station Street where the County Down Railway had its station and there we got on the train to Newtownards. There were about five stops on the way, at Bloomfield, Neill's Hill, Knock, Dundonald and Comber. Then we got the Ards Transport from Newtownards to Portavogie, hard tyres and no top. Can you imagine - bump, bump, bump all the way? It took over two hours for the whole journey and it's not much more than twenty miles from Belfast.'

The Belfast and County Down Railway Terminus on 19 April 1913.
There is only one motor vehicle in sight.
(Hogg Collection, Ulster Museum)

Ena's whole family went to a boarding house in Bangor, just twelve miles away.

'We went to Bangor and stayed in a house there for the whole summer. I used to walk to Ballyholme or round by where the Salvation Army played. Once I listened to a man tell about how he started drinking when he was only sixteen and I wondered why he was so silly as to tell everyone his business. Of course I was a wee girl and I was too young to know that he was giving his testimony!'

Annie's family could never afford a holiday and her father could not afford to spend time away from his shop. A day trip to Bangor is the only break she can recall. Because of the pressure of work, Johnny's mother was unable to take holidays but every summer she sent him to a relation's farm in Newtowncrommelin, a small village at the head of the Glens of Antrim.

Johnny: I could do all that a farmer could. There was a great spirit of helping each other on the farm. The flax was a very hard job. Flax was sold by the stone, so it was heavy work. During the war it was used to make plane wings.

Mary's family weren't able to take holidays: 'My parents had five children in seven and a half years, so they'd neither the time nor the money for such luxuries. With my father chopping and changing jobs we were always on the move anyway.'

John has vivid memories of being taken on day excursions and as a small boy the most exciting ones involved the *Titanic*:

'My father worked on the building of the *Titanic* and he was very, very proud to have done so. He continually talked about it and I got a pleasant surprise when he told me one day that he was going to take me down to see the great ship. This he did on a Sunday afternoon before it was launched. I saw the ship in the gantry and he explained to me how they would take the props away and it would slip down into the water.

About six months after that, I was only about five years old, he took me again to see it. It looked more like a ship; the funnels and the lifeboats were on and it was down in the finishing wharf. Then a few months after that I saw the ship again when we took the tramcar to Greencastle. I was with my mother and father and sister on that occasion and we saw it sailing away. There were thousands and thousands there to watch it being towed up the lough. When it reached the mouth of the lough, we heard the noise of the great propellors and men threw their caps in the air. It was a wonderful sight. Little did we think that we would never see the ship again.

When word came through that the ship had sunk, my father just couldn't believe it. In fact he broke down and cried like a child. Everybody had such an interest and were so proud of having built this great ship that people said would never sink. He was also saddened because of the men that went down. His foreman and manager and one or two others that he knew were amongst those that were lost. It was a sad occasion for the people of Belfast. There were about thirty people from Belfast that died and they put up a memorial in front of the City Hall. Nobody ever suggested that there was anything wrong with the ship. It was man's greed for fame, trying to make new records for speed. They had used a different route to take a shortcut.'

Teresa does not feel that she missed anything by being unable to afford holidays because her whole world was her family and the neighbours in Portaferry:

'Neighbours all helped each other then, lease-lend. Maybe one person had a sewing machine and they sewed the flour bags. We bought them for two shillings each and after they were bleached it took four joined to make a sheet. It always said 112lbs on the back. The fronts were different according to the brands and the one I can picture had a Red Indian on the front in red. They were used to make sheets or quilts or drying cloths or hippens [nappies], just about anything.

Neighbours had many a laugh doing things together; people were more decent in those days, there was more neighbourliness. Willie Bailey lived next door to us and after he lost his job he found it hard to make ends meet. The rent then was five shillings and five pence a month and the priest used to come up and give him half a crown. My mother would have given him the other half crown. On a Sunday when she made the dinner one of us was sent to the hedge that divided our gardens, to pass through a plate to Willie Bailey. He'd been a Protestant and then he became a Catholic. One Tuesday mother saw him and he wasn't looking too well and she said to him "Willie Bailey, when did you last eat?" "On Sunday," he told her. He was proud and hadn't wanted to tell. She was really cross and she said: "Willie Bailey, don't you ever do that again." She was with him when he died and all of us children went after the coffin. My mother tended him and he said she could have what was in the house when he went. But she said no and took nothing, she hadn't done it for that reason. That was the spirit of people then - decent and proud.'

CHAPTER SEVEN
RELIGION REMEMBERED

When asked about the religion of people at her school, Ena was sure that they were all the same religion because they all lived nearby. Norman, on the other hand, could not be sure that they were all the same religion as himself. 'You sat at a long desk in school and you had an inkwell in front of you. You might have Tommy Cassidy next to you. You knew he was Tommy Cassidy, but he could have been a Roman Catholic and you wouldn't have known and you wouldn't have cared. I just couldn't tell you if there were Catholics at my school. As I said, you didn't really play with the ones at school.'

Norman had previously explained when talking about school that there was no such thing as a playground at his school, so you went straight to school and straight home again and there was therefore no real playing with those in school.

Like Ena, Annie was sure that all the people at her school were the same religion, but she could not explain why she thought this. Once again Johnny was sure of his facts: 'At the National school I attended everyone was Catholic, but Ballymena Academy was a Protestant school. There was never any trouble and I played with all the boys there. The only time religion was ever mentioned was in a science lesson where we made distilled water. A boy in the class made a comment about holy water and the master brought him up to the front and gave him six of the best. That was the only incident in those two years. It's a pity that master hadn't been a politician!'

Mary could not be absolutely sure and thought that there might have been some Catholics at her school because it was quite swanky. John knew that there had only been Protestants at his National school because 'there was a separate Roman Catholic school. It was different at the Belfast Model, all religions went there and a Roman Catholic teacher on staff took separate religious classes.' Teresa's school had only Catholics because 'there was a Protestant school in Ann Street and a wee Presbyterian school for the ones who didn't go to our school.'

Everyone was adamant that people of different religions lived in their streets and they played together.

Ena: I played with Jews and Protestants, who were part of my own special group of friends because they lived near me.

Norman: My friends were everybody in the street, including Catholics. One child, Joe Nulty, a Catholic, was a very close friend and remained a friend for life.

Annie: We just all played together and you wouldn't have known about religion because we were all the same in them days.

Johnny: Everybody was a friend then and you just played with whomever was around. There was maybe a bit of dryness [coolness towards each other] around the 12th of July, but we all forgot it the next day.

Mary: You went out to play with anyone who lived in your street or went to your school. Some were Protestant and some were Catholic. I remember one family who lived on the Earlswood Road. Gunning they were called. I played with Rita Gunning and she used to say 'I am a Roman Catholic'. It made no difference. My brothers' chums were Catholic too and they stayed friends all their lives.

John: Roman Catholics lived on our street and we all played together. There was one very good family, McDermott, and Mrs. McDermott was a great friend of my mother's and she used to come down and chat in our house. They were very friendly. And the Barretts - they owned the pub on the corner of Distillery Street - we were friendly with them too. It seems funny now but we used to go and play in the Falls Park a lot. We also played in the Bog Meadows. You knew people were a different religion but it didn't seem to matter, you were able to manage then. People had more important things to worry about, T.B. was very rife in those days. Families were greatly affected and I knew one family that had two or three in it die. It was all around us. Everybody said it was because people were underfed but I couldn't see that because there were some very, very good families that I knew and they lost several. There were sanatoriums, Forster

Greens was one. Whiteabbey was another one but it was the finish. If you went there it was like going to Beaconfield cancer hospital today.

Teresa: We played with the ones from round about, the neighbours. Everybody was very neighbourly; we had the hedges worn down with going from one house to another. There were Protestant children too and we all played together. My mother wouldn't have cared and anyway she was too busy because there was T.B. in our house too. My brother, William James, brought it into the house. He died in 1907, then Thomas died in 1909. In the year my father died, 1913, my brother Patrick died of it too. In 1916 it took my sister Mary and then in 1917, the funeral I remember best, my brother Francis died. They didn't go into sanatoriums and I remember a lot of sickness in the house when they were being nursed. The story of Lazarus makes me cry and I suppose it's because I remember my mother's sadness when she was nursing them. My mother said, 'I reared them for the grave.' The oldest of her five children that died was Mary and she was only twenty-three. If anybody served their Purgatory in this life it was my mother. She never liked us to treat people differently for any reason. That might have been because her father, my grandfather Treacy, was a Protestant. My mother didn't talk of that much but she did say that, when she was small, her mother worried when she was taken to visit her father's people. Her mother thought they might try to proselytise her. My mother thought that was silly because we all worshipped the same God.

No one remembers ever being told that they could not play with someone because they were of a different religion. However, while Ena, Johnny, Mary, John and Teresa feel that it was the same everywhere then, Norman is not so sure.

Norman: I don't think everywhere was the same. There was always the Falls Road and there was always the Shankill Road, and in that area I wouldn't say it was the same because the Falls Road was always predominantly Catholic, though there were Protestant Churches on it, and the Shankill Road was much the same. In this area [east Belfast] it was okay.

OUR HEROES—IN MEMO

DUFFY—A tribute of love to the mem dear husband, S.P.O. Alexander T. D was lost at sea with H.M.S. Mary Ro on October 17, 1917; also his brother, Major Thomas Duffy, M.M., of the Forces, killed in action on August R.I.P.

There is in the wide, lone sea
A spot unmarked, but holy,
Where the one so dear to me
In his ocean bed lies lowly.

Still sadly missed by his loving Wif and two little Children, MOLLY
29 Mackey Street.
Also his Mother-in-law and Sister-in Brother-in-law,
Mrs. LEGGETT, ROBINA KE AND JOHN LEGGETT (t somewhere at sea).
18 Mackey Street.

O'HARA—October 16, 1918, at her residence, 14 Galway Street, Sarah, widow of James O'Hara. —R.I.P. Funeral arrangements later
"On her soul, sweet Jesus, have mercy."
Deeply regretted by her sorrowing Daughter and Sons, BRIDGET, JAMES, AND JOHN (the latter on active service).

O'NEILL—October 15, 1918, at his parents' residence, 16 Ormond Street, John, the youngest and dearly-beloved son of Charles and Isabella O'Neill.—R.I.P. His remains will be removed from above address on to-morrow (Friday), for interment in Milltown Cemetery.
On his soul, sweet Jesus, have mercy.
Deeply regretted by his Father, Mother, Sister, and Brothers.

PORTER—October 15th, 1918, at her parents' residence, 20 Bowness Street, Isabella, youngest and dearly-beloved daughter of John and Martha Porter. Her remains will be removed on to-morrow (Friday), at 2-30 p.m., for interment in City Cemetery. Friends will please accept this intimation.

I waited for the Lord my God,
And patiently did bear.

Deeply regretted by her sorrowing Father and Mother, JOHN AND MARTHA PORTER; also, her Sisters and Brothers-in-law, JEANNIE AND MAXWELL REID, MAGGIE AND WILLIAM KEARNS; also, her Brother and Sister-in-law, W. JOHN AND MARY PORTER.

SERGAI—October 14, 1918, killed in seaplane accident, Bennett Sergai, M.M.A. (formerly of Texas, U.S. America), second son of Harris Sergai and the late Mrs. Harris Sergai. His remains will be removed from his father's residence, 2 Lonsdale Street, Belfast, on to-morrow (Friday), at 10 a.m., for interment in Carnmoney Cemetery.

SOMERSET—October 16, 1918 (suddenly), at his residence, 32 Kenilworth Street, Newtownards Road, James, the dearly-beloved husband of Elizabeth Somerset. His remains will be removed from above address on Saturday, at 2.30 p.m., for interment in Knock Burying-ground. Friends will please accept this intimation.

God is good, He'll give me grace
To bear my heavy cross;
He is the only One Who knows
How bitter is my loss.

Deeply regretted by his sorrowing Wife and Family. Also his two Sons, Thomas and William (both on active service).
ELIZABETH SOMERSET.

THOMPSON—October 16, 1918, at his residence, "Old Warren," Lisburn, John Thompson. Funeral to Lisburn Cemetery on to-morrow (Friday), at 3 p.m. Friends will please accept this intimation.
Deeply regretted by his Brother-in-law and Nieces

There were no religious differences in the death columns of the *Belfast Telegraph* in 1918.

Since Ena lived on the Falls Road, Norman's views may just be supposition. She feels that religion wasn't really an issue and does not recall any negative comments in her home about other religions. This may have been because in his business life her father dealt with all religions. Some of her comments on the question further illuminate this.

Ena: We had a housekeeper called Mrs. Mortimer. She was a Protestant but that was only a name to us, just like Quakers. It didn't mean anything. I loved the Quakers; they were so good. Sometimes on Saturday, when I was at school, my father would send me round to deliver things to them. One day they asked would I like some dinner and I said 'I wouldn't mind, thank you.' They didn't give me anything and I couldn't understand. My father explained that I should just have replied 'yes' because Quakers didn't expect any other reply since it was wrong to say please or thank you to anyone but God. The next Saturday I just said 'yes' and they gave me a dinner, but it was meatballs and I'd never seen them before. They tasted funny so I hid them up the leg of my knickers and ran home. Everybody at home laughed when they fell out. I never said 'yes' again! Half-timers worked in the Falls Road mill and they were both Catholic and Protestant, it didn't matter. One of our Catholic friends got a job in a mill where they sang hymns all day long and my father said that was good because then they couldn't be gossiping about each other. There was no bigotry in my father. He went about with Billy Weir, who was in the 'Black', and many's a time my father waited for him after a march and Billy Weir took his sash off and they went for a drink together. [The 'Black' is the name given to the Royal Black Preceptory which was established in 1797 for the 'preservation of the Protestant religion.' It is less overtly political than the Orange order, but is so closely tied that membership of the Black is restricted to those who have passed a certain degree in the Orange Institution.]

Ena says that there were no places where people of her religion could not go. She says that her family went everywhere and to all the football matches. They used to visit people called McKinstry who lived in Lawnbrook Avenue, and they did all their shopping on the Shankill Road. Norman confirms this when talking about shopping and says that this attitude still prevailed in the thirties.

'I'm thinking of Lawnbrook Avenue and down at the bottom was Cooper Street and my future wife's family, who were Protestant, had a shop there for years. People from the Falls went to Anderson's shop on the Shankill because it was the only place to get a decent potato. Even in the thirties when I was a traveller, I had many Catholic customers on the Falls; George Wilson (his son Desmond is a well known priest today), the two Miss Galways, Mrs. Doherty, Sean Maguire and more, all on the Falls. When I

went into the Miss Galways, I always had to have a cup of tea. They were lovely ladies.'
Annie doesn't remember anyone ever thinking about not going places because of religion and is sure that cinemas and shopping were frequented by both religions. Johnny supports this view when talking about Ballymena.

Johnny: The main shops were all Protestant and the pubs were Catholic. There was no bigotry in any of them or in the ones in which we shopped. Prior to the passing of the Home Rule Bill, a crowd used to walk about with a Lambeg drum and flutes. They burned an effigy of John Redmond or Joe Devlin. They were just rabble and never bothered us. We always felt we could go anywhere.'

Mary, John and Teresa felt exactly the same way.

No religious bigotry emerges in any of the comments about religion.

Norman: I wasn't aware of what Catholics believed or what they were taught. It was just people went to Chapel, they were Catholic; people went to the Tabernacle, Central Hall, Ravenhill Presbyterian, they were Protestant. That was the difference. There were Protestant and Catholic churches on every main road and nobody thought twice about that. The great thing in connection with the churches was that they ran house parties, maybe in Hatton Drive or there was another house in Cyprus Avenue that I went to. There were Roman Catholics present because they knew somebody who was there too. We played postman's knock and other silly games and you got a lovely supper. It was another form of enjoyment.

Annie: We weren't allowed to play outside on a Sunday, so we played tents in the bedroom. One day some boys came outside and shouted in at us 'You're not allowed out cos your shoes are in the pawn!' We didn't really realise that there were differences because of religion, we just knew we went to different churches. I went to East End Baptist in Church Street morning and night and to Sunday School in the Iron Mission Hall. I was very good when I was a girl. My parents didn't go to church but they sent us. When I was very young I didn't like Sundays because we had no fun.

As the following letter, copied from the *Belfast News Letter* of 7 September 1916, indicates there were some who wanted Sundays to be observed strictly, and others who were so outrageous that they travelled on trains!

SABBATH OBSERVANCE TO THE EDITOR OF THE BELFAST NEWS-LETTER.

SIR - I am a Belfastman domiciled in a part of Ireland where, to put it mildly, the observance of the Sabbath is not too conspicuous a feature of the majority of the people. Almost every Sunday special trains are run with their full complements of patronisers of sports of different kinds. I have frequently reminded the folk in these parts how differently it is in the North, and that such things would not be approved or sanctioned there; but I have been wondering if I will have to hold my peace as far as the running of special trains is concerned, as I have recently observed a growing tendency in this direction in connection with Masonic services. Of course there is no comparison between these and Sunday sports, and I am in thorough sympathy with the aim and motive of these services; but surely it ought to be possible to have them without the running of special trains, which your journal informs us are largely availed of. By whom? Doubtless the members of the Masonic Order are amongst these, but is the number restricted to these? Whether or not, I hardly think it is a step in the right direction to encourage these special trains on Sunday.

Johnny: We all went to church on a Sunday. I was an acolyte in the church and I got up each morning to serve Mass. Various denominations had services in the workhouse and I went there with the priest on Sunday. I can still remember the sight of those poor people scrubbing floors. I knew that Catholics went to church more than Protestants and that only better-class Protestants went, but I viewed them more as denominations, not different religions.

Mary: My mother and father wouldn't have let you say anything about people of other religions. They'd had good neighbours on the farm in Tyrone and they had been different religions. In fact my father said that on the twelfth of July Catholics would have worked your farm for you if you were away enjoying yourself.

Teresa: On the twelfth of July James Merlin and his brother Sam used to get dressed up in their collarettes [the sashes worn by Orangemen] and went away to the Twelfth celebrations and met all the people and had a good day. Nobody said anything about it. Then they would have had something down in the school and some of the kids got walloped for going down to try to get tea. We knew they weren't Catholics, but nobody bothered about that.

As children, everyone except Mary was taught to say prayers at home. Ena and Teresa learned the Rosary and 'little hymns' while Norman had to say his prayers at night under supervision: 'Just a family prayer: God Bless Mum and Dad, Bertie, Ray and Tommy, aunts and uncles.' Annie was told to say her prayers each night and Johnny said the rosary with his family when his mother had the time. John's family always said prayers at night.

When asked how much religion meant to each of them as a child, they replied:

Ena: We got plenty of it; it was important. Things like, 'Who's your neighbour? Mankind of every description.'

Norman: As a child, it was a way of life. It was the only life I knew.

Annie: I just went because I was sent. You had to go dressed to church in them days with your hat and all.

Johnny: Religion didn't mean a great deal to me when I was young. Church was somewhere that most people went to but I suppose it did introduce us to the idea of 'them' and 'us'.

Mary: I suppose we weren't what you would call a very religious family. I don't remember praying much in those days.

John: We were all great church people and we went every Sunday. My grandparents were founder members of the old Christchurch and religion meant quite a lot to us all. While everybody mixed and played together it was not the done thing to go out with a person of a different religion, or get married to someone of a different religion.

Teresa: It was just a part of life but nothing was ever said against other religions. Mind you, I think all religions were based on fear then. It's much better now: children have no fear of the Bishop; he's like a big friend to them.

I asked if there was anywhere they couldn't go because of their religion when they were children, but all said no. Ena wasn't allowed to go to the park on her own, but only because there were men there. Norman was never permitted to go anywhere near bars or spirit grocers because drunks would be hanging around outside. Annie could not go to dances, or jigs as her father called them, but her brothers could. She also was not allowed to go to the second house of the pictures because all the boys went. The only place that Johnny recalls his mother refusing him permission to go to was the pool in the Braid river where people went to bathe. This was nothing to do with his religion but because the bathing was mixed and boys often wore their sisters' knickers! Mary was allowed to go anywhere because they were too well trained to want to go anywhere they shouldn't. John was warned against going near the bookies around the corner and it would have been unheard of to be in a public house. He was permitted to go to the spirit grocers for milk or butter. Teresa wasn't supposed to go into other churches but she did: 'I went into them all. I went into the vestry in the Church of Ireland one day and you know there was a chamber pot in the cupboard. I suppose it was in case the minister took short. I laughed, you never thought then that men of the cloth had to go to the toilet like ordinary people.'

CHAPTER EIGHT
MISSIONS REMEMBERED

Everyone went to missions of some description in their leisure time and the memories of these show that they were of greater significance to those who remember the decade than any political event. Missions were religious meetings and Norman's recollection of them is very vivid.

Norman: There was a mission in the Tab. [Baptist Tabernacle] every year of some description. Real take-ons [attempts to fool people] the whole lot of them. My Dad used to be raging at me every time when I used to say that. There was one fellow called Shakesby, a big strapping fellow - the great thing about missions was that they used to give their life story every Friday night and I remember this fellow telling how he was walking along somewhere in London and there was this place on fire and there was a man on a balcony shouting "help, help, help." And, he said, I told him to jump and he jumped and I caught him but we both hit the ground and I was on crutches for six months. I was told that I would never be able to do without them, but one night I was preaching in Nottingham and I got so excited that the two crutches fell to the floor and I said "Praise the Lord" and I never had to use them again.

I said to myself, what a cock and bull story. He was a real chancer. You also had to give a donation. That was another thing I couldn't see eye to eye with. They made their living out of it.

Then there was another fellow who came from Nottingham, by the name of Bakewell and I used to say he was well-baked before he came here. Missions were really popular. In the nineteen twenties there was a mission in Ravenhill Church and the men marched up to it from the shipyard and they couldn't get in the door quickly enough, so they took the pillars off. I saw that. That was the Reverend W.P.Nicholson's mission, a very famous man. I went with my mother once when I was a boy to hear one of his missions. The church was full and just as he started speaking two women came in late. They had hats with feathers on and Nicholson stopped speaking and said 'Let the peacocks sit down.' Everybody laughed. He liked to have a laugh at the start.

When I was young there was another lovely man. I can remember him well, he was sacred-looking, lovely white hair and lovely white beard. He was called Dr. Mountain and he was a gem. I absolutely adored him. I'm sure I went every night to hear him when I got my schoolwork done. Then there was a man who had his own hymnbook and I got it; it was lovely. He was called Arnold Young and he conducted the mission and sang his own songs. I remember one well.

We stand for the Bible, 'tis true.
God's word from beginning all through.
From its pages we trace
All the treasures of grace.
God's word from beginning to end.

Dear goodness, I loved him. He was a great singer too. My father expected me to go to the mission at least twice in the week. On one of the nights you heard the testimony and that could be a bit of a lark. At the end of the night you'd to put up your hand if you were going to give your life to God. If you did, you went up to the front and signed a card. There were two hymns they played as you went up. One was 'Just as I am without one plea' and the other was 'Almost persuaded now to be thine.' The next night they waved the cards in the air to show how many souls had been saved the night before. I always wondered did they get paid for the number of cards they had at the end of the week.

My mother used to walk me down Frank Street and past the Salvation Army Hall which was opposite the Picturedrome on the Mountpottinger Road. Their band always used to play opposite the Mount every Sunday night from half past six to seven. And I was intrigued with their music and I used to say to my father 'Can I go down to hear the Army?' and my father said 'Well, you be back for your church.' Well it very often happened that I walked down to the Hall with the band and went in with them. I got totally involved, so much so that I got to know a whole lot of people my own age and it was a completely different outlet because Major Fletcher was the Army officer and he was a brilliant character. He used to have cinema shows on a Monday night and I had to read the captions for the pictures that went up, moving pictures. I had to sit at a wee table with a candle and read the story as it came up on the screen, that was my job and I loved it. My dad didn't mind when that happened.

Ena too went to missions and not always in her own church. She had already said, when talking about church activities, that there was a mission in the church every year around Lent and "they thumped that pulpit and you thought you were in Hell'. At the other missions she attended the speakers would have been Protestant.

Ena: I used to go to missions in the Grosvenor Hall and in the Assembly Buildings. I also loved to go and listen to the preachers on the Custom House steps. Mr. Pimley was one of the preachers. One night in the Assembly Buildings there was a man preaching and there were soldiers there, right up at the front; it was during the war. The preacher told how his granny was in Hell because she had smoked while she was alive and smoking was a great sin. A bit later, but before he had finished talking, the soldiers got up to leave. I suppose they'd to be back in barracks for a certain time. They'd to walk right down from the front and as they left the preacher shouted that they'd go to Hell for leaving before the end. One of the soldiers shouted back 'If you give us a couple of fags, we'll give them to your granny.' I never forgot that. There was more humour in those days.

We would have gone to missions anywhere. We never thought of them as being Catholic or Protestant. They were a night out and sometimes you got a laugh like I just told you. And the boys telling their testimony could be good fun, all how they'd taken drink or smoked and had seen the light. The preacher always told you that you'd go to Hell and he banged and shouted a lot, just like the Lenten missions. And then he said he could save you from Hell if you did what God said. And sometimes he told good stories or there was singing. We went anywhere. There were films in some of them too. I think there were films in the Grosvenor Hall. At the Lenten missions we always knew which sermon would be on each night so it wasn't as much fun. Still, it was an excuse for a new hat for the closing night. You just had to have a new hat for the last night.

Annie enjoyed missions just as much as Ena and Norman:

'I would have gone to missions in any of the churches round about. I wouldn't have gone into town because I didn't know it well, but I liked getting my hat on to go to missions because I felt dressed up. They were great nights. When I was eighteen or nineteen I was saved at a mission and it changed my way of life because I stopped going to the pictures. It was at one of the Reverend Nicholson's missions that I was saved. He was a great evangelist.'

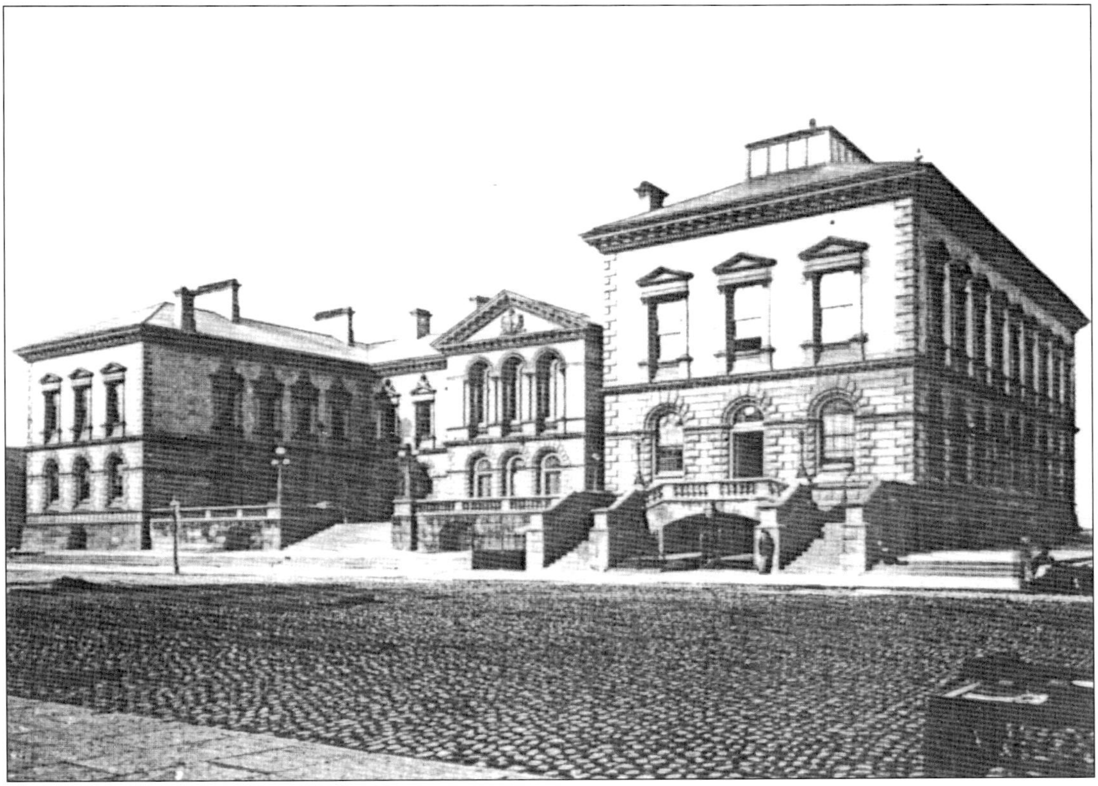

The Belfast Custom House, opened in 1857, is Belfast's grandest example of the adaptation of the style of Italian Renaissance merchants' buildings to Victorian mercantile purposes. Open-air services were held on these steps from the late nineteenth century.

(Lawrence Collection, courtesy of the National Library of Dublin)

Johnny says that officially he went only to church missions which were held each year but he used to enjoy listening to preachers on the street.

Johnny: A whole crowd would gather round these men who had huge booming voices. They would rant on about the perils of eternal damnation and how you could save yourself from it. I wasn't afraid, it was more like street theatre.

Mary also heard Nicholson preach: 'I went once to see Nicholson in Megain church on the Newtownards Road. He'd this mission there and we all went down, a whole crowd of us and we put up our hands when he

Open air gospel preaching in Belfast in 1913

asked who wanted to be saved. Nicholson must have given our names into our own churches for he'd asked where we came from. The next thing that happened was that Barton, the senior minister in our church, landed down one morning to the house. I hadn't told my mother anything about it for the others in the family would have made fun of me. It was because of Nicholson really that we changed church. Dr. Agnew, a young minister from Moira, he'd a thing in the *Telegraph* one night advertising a talk 'Christ or Nicholson?' My brother was very close to my mother - I was my father's girl - and he said to my mother 'I think we'll go and see what he has to say about this Nicholson.' Agnew turned them completely against Nicholson and our family changed to Dr. Agnew's church. It was the non-subscribing Presbyterian church in York Street. Nicholson didn't have a church of his own. Some people said he caused trouble.'

When he was a boy, John listened to W.P. Nicholson preach too. Later on he went with all the men from the shipyard. They went directly from work to wherever Nicholson was.

Teresa wasn't very keen on missions and sometimes they made her feel guilty:

'The missions were always in October and the dark nights made them even more scary. It was all Hell and damnation and flames and I was terrified. A woman called Mrs. Savage lived at the end of the road and she read the cups. She always came into our house and was very nosy. She would poke around in the tea leaves and then she would say 'I see a letter coming' and she would ask my mother 'Have you any idea what that letter would be?' At this point my mother would say to me 'take that bucket and go up to the pump.' I would say 'But it's half full' and my mother would say 'Go up anyway and get fresh.' That was to get rid of me but I knew what they were doing. One night at the mission they were wild against fortune-telling and said it was a sin to have a fortune-teller in the house. I thought we would be struck down there and then but when I looked up at my mother she didn't seem concerned. Afterwards she said that it had been a great mission and she had enjoyed it. The next time Mrs. Savage came she still got brought in.'

Missions appear to have been another form of entertainment for many people before 1920, though Norman makes a distinction. He says that he saw them as an outlet and viewed cinemas as entertainment. This is quite consistent with his Baptist background and it is interesting that he viewed both missions and the Salvation Army as outlets and remembers both so vividly. Missions were religious theatre and people looked forward to the performances which they can recall so accurately after nearly eighty years. Such performances either supplemented or replaced commercial theatres and cinemas.

That missions were a piece of religious theatre is borne out by the fact that what my informants recall so vividly are the entertaining aspects of the missions which they attended, the pun on the preacher's name, the smart reply of the soldier to the preacher, the far-fetchedness of the stories, the physical appearance of the preacher and his singing ability, and the melodrama of dark nights and Hell's flames.

The church in Portaferry in 1918 when Teresa attended missions.
(W.A. Green Collection, Ulster Folk and Transport Museum)

The format of the missions which all attended, in the Assembly Buildings, the Grosvenor Hall, the Custom House steps, the street or their own churches, seems to have followed the pattern of De Liguori's Directive of 1890 for Catholic missions. This called for an argument which established the nature of sin, the listener's sinful state, the awfulness of the Hell that awaited the sinner, the Salvation of Jesus Christ and the Church's possession of the sacraments through which such a salvation of Jesus Christ could be achieved. This format seems to have been used, regardless of denomination, in the remembered Ireland before partition.

CHAPTER NINE

POLITICS and PARTITION REMEMBERED

Ena is absolutely sure that her father took no interest in politics and never belonged to any club, society or political organisation. Norman's father was 'a very hot unionist' but he did not belong to any organisations.

Norman: There was never an Orangeman amongst us. Despite this my father walked me, in my gutties [canvas shoes], from Ravenhill Avenue to the Lisburn Road to see them.

Annie describes her father as being 'very loyal. I remember him going to the Old Princess Picturehouse when Sir Edward Carson was training the men there. They had belts and all and they had to march and they had wooden guns. That was the Ulster Volunteers.'

Johnny's mother had neither the time nor the inclination to be interested in politics and no one in his home belonged to any political organisation. He says that there was no point in voting anyway because they lived in the Mid-Antrim constituency of the Imperial parliament.

Ena has no recollection of her father ever going to vote but Norman thinks he remembers his father voting. He doesn't know what he voted, but he is sure that it would have been unionist. Annie has a vivid memory of her father voting: 'My father voted and he must have usually voted unionist all times before, you see, because I remember one time he had a brother who went up for election and his brother was Labour. This time he voted for his brother and a man shouted down the street at him "Go on, ye old turncoat".'

Not only did Mary's father vote - he was a Labour man - he was also a member of the party and went to meetings in Victoria ward. Her mother had strong views in support of Labour and passed tales of her childhood on to her children.

Mary: My mother often talked about her childhood in the Clogher valley. She said about the place where she was born that English people took the land and her father had to pay rent for it in November. He wouldn't touch his hat to them and because of this he was called a 'Home Ruler.' My mother was friendly with a cook in one of the big houses and heard all the tales about them. They built big houses in the valley and my mother talked about them, Killycarnon, Favoroyal and Killybrick. She knew all the names. There were churches built inside their grounds and one even had cushioned seats for the Moutray family. My mother didn't think it was right for the rich to take what they wanted.

John is sure of his father's views: 'He didn't belong to any of these orders but he was a staunch unionist; he always went to vote. My father was one of the Ulster Volunteer Force and we always had a picture of Sir Edward Carson in the hall.'

Teresa's mother was a regular voter: 'It was an outing for her. She probably voted for a Catholic party but she didn't want to be involved in anything political. The grown-ups didn't talk too much about it to us but I know she didn't want anything to do with the Sinn Feiners because one night Gerard was singing in the garden, it was a come-all-ye, and my mother told me to tell him not to sing it in case anyone thought he was one of them.'

No one ever attended a rally as a child, even though many pro- and anti-Home Rule demonstrations were held at the time. Nor did they ever consider people of another religion to be a different nationality. When asked what nationality they thought themselves to be then, they all said that when they were children, they just thought of themselves and everyone else as Irish.

Ena: What else could we all have been?

Norman: I certainly knew that I wasn't English .

Annie: We just knew that we lived in Ireland and were from it.

Johnny: I knew there were at least two religions when I was a child but I never thought of them as different nationalities. We were all the same in that respect. We lived in Ireland and Dublin was the capital, even if it meant little to us. All our books told us that.

Mary: We never considered we were anything but Irish.

John: We didn't think of the country as divided before. I can even remember going to hear de Valera speak at a meeting near our church.

Teresa: We lived in Portaferry in the County of Down, Ireland. We were all Irish.

That changed on 23 December 1920 when the Government of Ireland Act established a six-county parliament and administration in the North of Ireland. Ena was almost sixteen, Norman was eleven, Annie was seventeen, Johnny was two months past his sixteenth birthday, Mary was twelve, John was almost thirteen and Teresa was eleven. Yet not one remembers the Act of Partition as being of any great importance to them. They can recall events which occurred then, but did not see partition itself as having any great significance. They all remember the violence that took place afterwards, though they said they didn't really associate it with the political events. They knew that something in their world had changed and, when talking about it, the word 'sectarian' enters their accounts for the first time.

Ena: Our business was nearly all across the water anyway so we didn't think it would make any difference. My father said that Ireland was always like a jealous woman and a jealous woman never changes. Partition wouldn't change her either. The unrest, as I remember it, came when I was in my mid-teens. The B Specials were specifically designed as a sectarian force; they were not well received in British Liberal or Labour circles. The reason for their all Protestant, all British content was that Catholics would not join anyway. Their means of keeping law and order was very brutal, the Black and Tans made 1920 a year of terror on the streets, killing and maiming and taking pot-shots at Catholic people. I well remember the aftermath of their raids and the awful fear and atmosphere and the lack of trust. Two families I knew were completely wiped out, murdered in their homes.

There was curfew and the penalty of breaking that was certain death. I was at an age when I was home early anyway so it didn't affect me really but I was very aware of it. Sadly this started fear of the 'other side' and this is so to this day.

Norman: Being a young lad, I can remember my dad taking me to Upper Ann Street to see King George and Queen Mary. I was quite unaware and indeed not interested why they were here, but I can well remember when we got to Upper Ann Street it was well nigh impossible to see the royals because we had great big six foot plus policemen in great pointed hats and soldiers with fixed bayonets standing so close we could barely get a good view. However I was told some time later that the whole affair had something to do with the opening of the Northern Ireland parliament.

A few things stand out in my memory. First we had the arrival of the Black and Tans; they were a fearsome lot. They wore black uniforms and had their revolvers strapped round their right upper leg between the knee and the thigh. They shot first and asked questions later. The second thing was curfew; that meant we all had to be indoors by nine p.m. This was very hard to take, especially on a warm summer's evening when we could have been enjoying ourselves in the Ormeau Park. The soldiers came round in tall cage vans, that means there was a v-shaped cage covering the top of the van with a slit of about twelve inches to allow a gun to jut out. One incident comes to mind, we had a regiment of Seaforth Highlanders stationed in Belfast and one of their officers was shot dead in Arthur Square and as a result the soldiers went out for revenge and were really ruthless.

At that time we had what were known as spirit grocers where you could buy bread, butter, sugar, jam and then have a glass of beer or any kind of intoxicating liquor you desired. There was one such on Rosebery Road [east Belfast] who had been in the business for a long time. He was known as Lukie Clark, a Roman Catholic, and one night a crowd came and put all his furniture on the street and set it alight. Then they got the beer barrels and rolled them down the street. They put him out of business and I have no idea what became of him. [Norman said this with great sadness.]

I was going to a meeting with my mother one night and when we crossed from Cherryvale Street on to the Beersbridge Road shots rang out. We saw two men running out of the pub at the corner of Pottinger Street after having shot dead the man behind the counter, also a Catholic. Mum and I made for home again. After this I remember my brother making a sling, a baton-shaped wooden truncheon with a large piece of lead placed in the top. These were made by all and sundry where he worked and carried for protection against sectarian attacks.

Annie: I can well remember the curfew. Sometimes the children would be out in the street and when the soldiers came along everybody ran inside and closed their doors because they were so afraid. We thought the soldiers would shoot us and they did shoot innocent people. Partition? I never really thought of us as becoming two countries, we were still bits of the same country.

I'd another reason for not forgetting the curfew. We all thought my brother was really lucky because he was wounded during the war before the 1st of July 1916, that was the Battle of the Somme and he missed the battle because he was sent home. The curfew showed he wasn't lucky at all. My sister-in-law, Bella, died because of the curfew. She was out for the day on a boat-trip. Some neighbours asked her to go on a daytrip on a big boat which a man called Proudfoot had. When they came back, they couldn't land at the Queen's bridge because of the curfew so they had to get in the wee boats and row to Sydenham.

Queuing for the ferry boats on the river Lagan in 1908.
This rowboat ferry plied across the river for many years.
(Hogg Collection, Ulster Museum)

Well the boat Bella was in capsized and she held on to a man and pulled him down with her. Her wee girl drowned too. At that time my brother was on the boats and he was in Calcutta, so he couldn't get home. His wife and child were dead and buried and he never saw them.

There were two other brothers and this was a Saturday night and they'd had a drop of drink on them. Now mind they weren't drunk, but they'd called in to see my mother and she told them to hurry home or they'd be caught in the curfew. On their way home somebody told them what had happened and they went to see. The bulkies [security men at the harbour] wouldn't let them through and they pushed them over, but by the time they got to the water Bella had been pulled out dead. They didn't get the wee girl's body for three weeks. If the curfew hadn't been on, they could have landed at Queen's Bridge, you see. The curfew caused their death in a way. I remember that my other brother came to the house and my daddy was in bed and he told him that Bella had been drowned. They could hear the screams of the people as they went down.

Johnny: There had been controversy before the war and there was the revival of the Irish language. One of my National school teachers went to Donegal to learn Irish but we viewed it no differently from somebody going off to learn any skill. I can remember the U.V.F. marching and gunrunning. I saw one of the guns, it had 'For God and Ulster' on it. Ballymena was mainly Protestant, yet we all got on. When Home Rule started, I went to see Edward Carson at Fairhill. James Craig walked beside him.

I was at St. Malachy's during partition but I didn't really see it as of great importance, nor did I believe that we were two different peoples. What was more important to me then was that a fellow who sat beside me was killed. Only then did some of my classmates say that you could never trust the English, I thought that was shocking because my memories of the war telegrams were so vivid and we'd all fought together then.

Mary: I have few memories of partition, I suppose because I wasn't really interested. We didn't go to see the King and Queen. My brother was at Tech [Belfast Technical College] and there was shooting all around there one night. My mother was worried and went over to bring him home. I don't think there were any soldiers around Cheviot Avenue where we lived, but there was curfew. One night my granny gave us tickets to a show in the Ulster Hall and my chum Jeanette and I went. That was during the curfew. Another friend's father was a sergeant and he'd had to move with his family from Strandtown to the police station behind the Tech. After the show Jeanette and I decided to go and see this friend, Ena, at the barracks. We didn't know it was after half past ten and the police ended up looking for us. That sort of thing was more important to me at the time than who ruled the country.

John: I can remember the severe rioting after partition, the curfew at night and the soldiers behind barricades at the end of our street. That was when the Belfast Model was burned down. I was in the guard of honour with the Boys' Brigade when George V came to open the parliament. My family wanted to stay with Britain but we didn't want the country divided.

Teresa: I don't remember much about partition, we were more interested in what was on the table. But the Sinn Feiners became very active afterwards in Portaferry. There was a house across the lough owned by the de Rossa's and they set fire to it. Father Brady condemned them and my mother didn't like him walking about on his own after that and she made my brothers walk him up the road. Half of the Sinn Feiners ended up in the Argenta, the prison ship on the lough. I don't think any of them could swim!

Norman talked a lot about the loss of trust and agreed with the other's views. Everyone felt that the violence of the time, and not the political events, had made trust disappear. The discussion made Norman think about the meaning of trust and he said he had many thoughts on the subject while lying in bed at night. He wrote the following to me.

TRUST

Trust is a very strong word and well defined in the dictionary. When you take each letter, as I will endeavour to do, the result is soul-searching.

T - Truthfulness
R - Responsibility
U - Understanding
S - Sincerity
T - Tolerance

This is a very high mountain to climb with lots of loose boulders on the way. Lack of trust forms a good part of our lives, as a nation and indeed of the world. But climb we will because it is always better to have tried. Perhaps one day the trust that people of my age once knew will return.

Norman Douglas, 1996, aged 87

CHAPTER TEN
1910-1920 REVISITED

The picture painted by traditional historians of the period 1910 to 1920 is of Ulster as a province in turmoil. Huge demonstrations against Home Rule took place in the early part of the decade and there were many displays of strength by unionists, including the well-known signing of the Covenant by almost half a million people. Catholics were attacked by Protestants and vice versa, and armed groups of volunteers grew up on each side. World War I interrupted the hostilities as both sides fought a common enemy, although some of those left at home continued to plan an uprising against British rule in Ireland. Following the end of the war, political hostilities continued with sections of Ireland becoming even more polarised; violence increased and martial law had to be imposed. Finally at the end of 1920 the Better Government of Ireland Act received royal assent and Ireland was divided into a six-county part of the United Kingdom, and a twenty six-county country. Sectarian warfare broke out in Belfast.

Throughout these traditional history books there are only glimpses of a different Ireland. The fact that 'Ulster Day' passed with no more arrests than usual indicates that the level of violence was not heightened at that time and, although there might have been a little unpleasantness after the football match between Distillery and Celtic, the simple occurrence of the match on that day highlights the way in which normal, day to day life was operating.

The article written by Patrick Pearse shows that even someone who would later take part in the Easter Rising in Dublin saw the English as the enemy and not his fellow Protestant countrymen. The poem, published in the *Irish News* on the outbreak of the war, confirms that Pearse was not the only one who saw most inhabitants of the island as fellow-countrymen. The joint response to the war by both nationalists and unionists shows how quickly the people could unite in the face of a common enemy. The following article from the *Irish News* on 10 August 1914 aptly corroborates this.

NATIONAL AND ULSTER VOLUNTEERS MARCH TOGETHER

> The Ulster Volunteers and Irish National Volunteers united in Omagh on Friday night in giving a most hearty send-off to the final draft of the Army Reserve of the Royal Inniskillings, who left the town about half-past nine o'clock, and a scene of unparalleled description was witnessed when the procession of both bodies of Volunteers and military marched through the town together .... Subsequently, as both bodies of Volunteers paraded the town, they met one another and respectfully saluted.
>
> (Quoted by Bardon)

Nationalists and unionists, both were now 'the lads', and the Irish Recruiting Council capitalised on that fact and recruited volunteers from all parts of the country throughout 1918.

October 1918

IRISH RECRUITING COUNCIL

ENQUIRY & RECRUITING OFFICE

FOR THE NAVY, ARMY & AIR FORCE

NUMBER of MEN ACCEPTED for VOLUNTARY SERVICE

KEEP THE CLOCK HANDS MOVING

OUR RECRUITING EFFORT.

58 TO MAKE FIRST 10,000.

The following are the figures up to noon to-day:—Belfast, 58; Dublin, 26; Cork, 5; Limerick, 0; Waterford, 27; Omagh, 20; Galway, 6; Armagh, 2; Mullingar, 2; Sligo, 2.

The total in each area since June 1 is as follows:—Belfast, 3,710; Dublin, 2,343; Cork, 705; Limerick, 543; Waterford, 735; Omagh, 876; Galway, 209; Armagh, 322; Mullingar, 327; Sligo, 172. All told—9,942.

A STEADY ADVANCE.

IRISH TROOPS IN ACTION.

2,000 PRISONERS AND MANY GUNS.

The Special Correspondent of the Press Association at Correspondents' Headquarters of the British Army in France, writing on Wednesday afternoon, says:—Steadily our troops are coming up to the line of the Scheldt, linking up the few bridgeheads and footholds which have already been established along the western bank. The fighting of this morning has considerably extended our front along this waterway, which is mainly interesting because it had been suggested as a probable line of the German rally. To-day's battle has been very difficult to follow, because the conflict, beginning along a connected front, disintegrated into a series of local struggles. Thus, on the front between Valenciennes and Tournai, the Forêt de Raismes deflected the fighting below St. Amand. Bruay, about three miles north, and slightly east of Valenciennes, was reached by our troops, and Bleharies was also taken in spite of heavy machine-gun fire, coming from across the stream.

The country, over a wide area around where the Canal de Conde joins the Escout, is intersected by a perfect network of little waterways, which renders it very marshy, and extremely difficult for troops to advance across against deliberate defence.

Between Le Cateau and Sclesmes we are approaching the thick Mormal Forest. Under such conditions it is obvious that the news coming back from the 30-mile front must be scrappy and disconnected, so that a good deal of piecing together is necessary to gather anything approaching a connected understanding of what is happening.

We are drawing into long-range artillery reach of both Mons and Maubeuge, which are very vital points on the German communications, and it does not seem unduly optimistic to predict that in the near future the British troops will be beyond any line of French soil they have yet trodden in this war.

The battle of to-day is very similar in the character of the fighting to its predecessors of the past ten days. That is to say, it is almost wholly a struggle of infantry against machine gun resistance. The nature of the country is unfavourable to the employment of tanks, and even the moving up of guns is often a feat of considerable difficulty. Moreover, I gather that the tendency is to keep our columns as mobile as is practicable. Sappers are playing a great part in the present phase of field warfare, and are doing wonderful work in the renewal of destroyed bridges, the detection and removal of death traps, and the general maintenance of communications. But it is the infantry who are carving out the victory—battalions from the English shores, the Scottish heather, the Welsh hills, and the soft emerald levels of Ireland.

As this newspaper article shows, soldiers from all over Ireland were Irish troops and distinct from English, Welsh and Scottish soldiers on 24 October 1918.

When World War I ended on 11 November 1918 the rejoicings were the same for both religious groups which had lost equal numbers. Bardon recounts how people in Belfast poured out of the mills, city-centre strores and workshops when they heard the news of the armistice and produced 'a display of enthusiasm, amounting almost to emotionalism, on the part on the part of the public such as has never been witnessed in this city.' He also tells how mill girls swept down the Falls Road 'to the accompaniment of lively choruses while Irish flags of green and gold mingled with the Stars and Stripes and flags of the Allies.'

The people of Belfast were once again united in 1919, this time in the demand by workers for a forty-hour week. All the shipyard men, the gas workers and the electricity station workers downed tools and subsequently trams could not run, linen workers were laid off, the Ropeworks was closed down and there was a bread shortage. In this strike, all workers had similar aims and the strike was broken only by the occupation of the gasworks and electricity station by the army.

In 1920 Catholic workers were indeed expelled from the shipyard, but the fact that they had been reinstated after their expulsion in 1913, had remained at work for the rest of the decade, had taken part in the armistice celebrations and in the strike of 1919, suggests that, for the ordinary workman of Belfast, the divisions of the time were not as great as living through the subsequent period might lead one to believe.

As can be seen from newspaper advertisements, the number of pastimes in the decade was enormous and people had a wide variety to choose from. Apart from cinemas those living during 1910 to 1920 could have participated in the following events and clubs (which are only some of those which took place):

> Victoria Wheelers Valse Classes, Whist Drives, Flower Shows, Archeology Society Meetings, Musical Competitions, Belfast Natural History and Philosophical Society Meetings, Celtic Park Dog Racing, Lambeg Dog Racing, Rifle Shooting, Ulster Angling Association, National Cross Country Championship, Badminton Internationals, Billiards, Racing at Windsor,

Gymnastics, Co. Down Hunt Steeplechase, Athletics, Chess Clubs, Aquatic Festival, Ping-Pong, Athletic Carnival, Gaelic Athletics, Whippets, Homing Pigeon Clubs, Football, Rugby, etc.

All the newspapers examined reported mostly the same amusements, sporting events and news from the whole of Ireland. The following amusements advertised in The *Irish Times* in 1918 look unusual when, as we now know, partition was only two years away. Royal and war related activities dominate and the forthcoming George Bernard Shaw lecture looks intriguing.

Next Week, "GENERAL POST."
Play that drew all London to Haymarket Theatre.

GAIETY THEATRE.

Under the Distinguished Patronage of His Excellency The Lord Lieutenant, Who has Graciously Signified His Intention of being Present.

"OUR DAY" FUND MATINEE,
TO-DAY, COMMENCING 2.30.
Mrs. GREER presents the CURRAGH PLAYERS in
"COOK,"
Jerome K. Jerome's Funniest Play. First time in Ireland.
MR. MILTON ROSMER
As John Parable, and
MISS IRENE ROOKE
In her Original Part, as Played at the Kingsway Theatre, London.
Preceded by the Famous Sketch, "A SISTER TO ASSIST 'ER." Played by Mr. WALLACE LUPINO and Mr. J. RICHARDSON.
Also Mrs. Noble Johnson, Miss Barlow, Miss Vigors, Mr. Deacon, and Mr. Chris. Sylvester.
PRICES AS USUAL. BOOKING NOW.

EMPIRE THEATRE.

6.50.............TWICE NIGHTLY.............9.0
WALTER McNALLY OPERA CO.
TO-NIGHT—"TROVATORE."
Teresa Owens, Lucy Doyle, Florrie Ryan, Thos. J. Bevan, HARRY O'DEMPSEY, Jay Ryan, W. F. Toolan, Cyril Quinn.
Friday, Lurline; Saturday, Bohemian Girl. Monday, Maritana; Tuesday, Trovatore.
BOOK YOUR SEATS .... 'Phone 824.

MATINEE,
SATURDAY, THE NINETEENTH INST.,
IN AID OF THE
"LEINSTER" DISASTER FUND.

THE WALTER McNALLY OPERA CO. WILL PRESENT
"LURLINE."
PRICES:—STALLS, 5/- ....CIRCLE, 3/-
BOX OFFICE OPEN 11 to 6. TEL. 824.

ABBEY THEATRE.

TO-NIGHT, AT 8.15.
MATINEE SATURDAY, 2.30.
"THE WHITEHEADED BOY,"
A Comedy in Three Acts, by LENNOX ROBINSON.
Miss MAIRE O'NEILL as "AUNT ELLEN."
Mr. FRED. O'DONOVAN as "JOHN DUFFY."
Booking at Theatre. 'Phone 3268.
SUNDAY, 20th OCTOBER, AT 8.15,
Mr. G. B. SHAW
Will Lecture on "EQUALITY."
Admission .... 2/-, 1/6, 1/-, 6d.
Booking at Theatre.

TIVOLI 7 o'c., 9 o'c. Tel. 4125. TIVO

W. H. PROWSE,
The Exceptional Entertainer.
POWER AND BENDON,
"I'm only an Apprentice."
Charles Ancaster. Emillion Bros.
And Full Variety Company.

KINGSTOWN PAVILION

TO-DAY, TO-MORROW, and SATURDAY,
"FOR ALL ETERNITY."
A Superb British Production, introducing the famo[us] old song of Mascheronis. A Dramatic Play [of] heart-gripping appeal and great artistic mer[it].
Showing each day at 4.15, 6.35, and 9.5.
BY SPECIAL REQUEST, we are also showing
SCENES OF THE DISASTER TO
SS. "LEINSTER."
which will be screened at 4.5, 6.30, and 8.50.
Supported by Usual Splendid Programme.

FROM 3. KINGSTOWN PICTURE HOUSE. TILL 10.20

TO-DAY, TO-MORROW, and SATURDAY,
"THE MYSTERIOUS MR. TILLER."
A Detective Story with a Novel Ending.
SCENES OF THE DISASTER OF R.M.S. LEINSTER.

ROYAL HORTICULTURAL SOCIETY.

WINTER SHOW,
FRUIT, VEGETABLES,
FLOWERS, FORESTRY
LORD IVEAGH'S COVERED YARD, EARLSFORT TERRACE.
Admission To-day, 17th, 12 to 4, 1/- (Tax included).

WOUNDED SOLDIERS' HANDICRAFT COMMITTEE.

EXHIBITION AND SALE OF WORK
DONE BY WOUNDED SOLDIERS
Of the Hospitals in the Dublin District
Will be held in the
GREAT HALL, ROYAL HOSPITAL, KILMAINHAM,
ON FRIDAY, NOVEMBER 1st.
MILITARY BAND will be in attendance.
The Sale will be opened by His Excellency the Lord Lieutenant at 2.30 p.m.
Entrance Tickets can be obtained at 51 Dawson st.
ENTRANCE 1/-. TEA EXTRA.

The only differences which are immediately obvious in newspapers are that the Gaelic Athletic results were printed only in the *Irish News* and the Clonard Picture House did not advertise in the *Belfast Telegraph* or *News Letter.*

The choice of picture houses increased dramatically as the decade progressed and in Belfast alone twenty-seven new ones were opened between 1910 and 1920. These were huge establishments and they were built in all areas. The Clonard, Falls Road, opened in 1913 and had 1100 seats, the Coliseum, Grosvenor Road, 1911, had 1200 seats, the Picturedrome, Mountpottinger Road, 1911, had 1000 seats, and the Princess, Newtownards Road, 1910, had 1200 seats. By 1920 there were 22,902 additional seats in Belfast where picturegoers could go. Often films were shown in episodes to keep the audience returning.

GRAND OPERA HOUSE
TO-NIGHT, at 7.15. MATINEE, FRIDAY.
The Successful Comedy,
"THE MAN FROM TORONTO."

ROYAL CINEMA.
CONTINUOUS PERFORMANCE, 1.30 to 10.30.
"HANDS UP" (5 Parts).
"THE TENDERFOOT" (5 Parts).
MAY REID,
With a remarkable Soprano Voice,
Daily, at 4 and 8.30.

PANOPTICON—TO-DAY.
RUTH STONEHOUSE, in **"FOLLOW THE GIRL,"**
A Fine Western Story with a Spy Element and some Splendid Riding.
Episode 6 of "CAB No. 13."
TO-DAY and TO-MORROW "THE SIGN OF THE CROSS" will be shown,
BUT NOT ON SATURDAY.
MONDAY NEXT:—"THE MARRIAGE AUCTION."

Many of the sporting events were between teams from differing parts of Ireland or of different religions. It was normal for Belfast Celtic to play Linfield and it is interesting that even in 1918 this could occur without acrimony. In international games sportspeople, such as rugby players, football players, boxers and other athletes were, like today, still competing for Ireland at the end of 1919. Other sporting activities were popular with either religion, and clubs existed in all parts of the city.

The same plays, films and variety concerts were watched by people of both religions and Charlie Chaplin was obviously a common favourite. With a booming post-war economy, the ordinary people had more to spend on luxuries such as cinemas, fish and chips and Italian ice-cream and all such outlets had expanded by the end of the decade.

In general all the newspapers studied reported news events in a non-divisive way and only towards the end of the decade did the word sectarian become part of the language used.

Arrival in New York of the Ulster Delegation :
'the mission is not sectarian.'
(*Belfast Telegraph*, 6 December 1919)

Readers of the *Ireland's Saturday Night*, the *Belfast Telegraph*, the *Irish News*, and the *Belfast News-Letter* alike learned of all the same leisure activities for both religions and read the same news reports from all around Ireland. They may have read of various rallies for or against Home Rule but these were given no more importance than was the 'Women's Patriotic Crusade for Prohibition During the War.'

In fact the size of an advertisement for this crusade would make it appear to be the event of the decade!

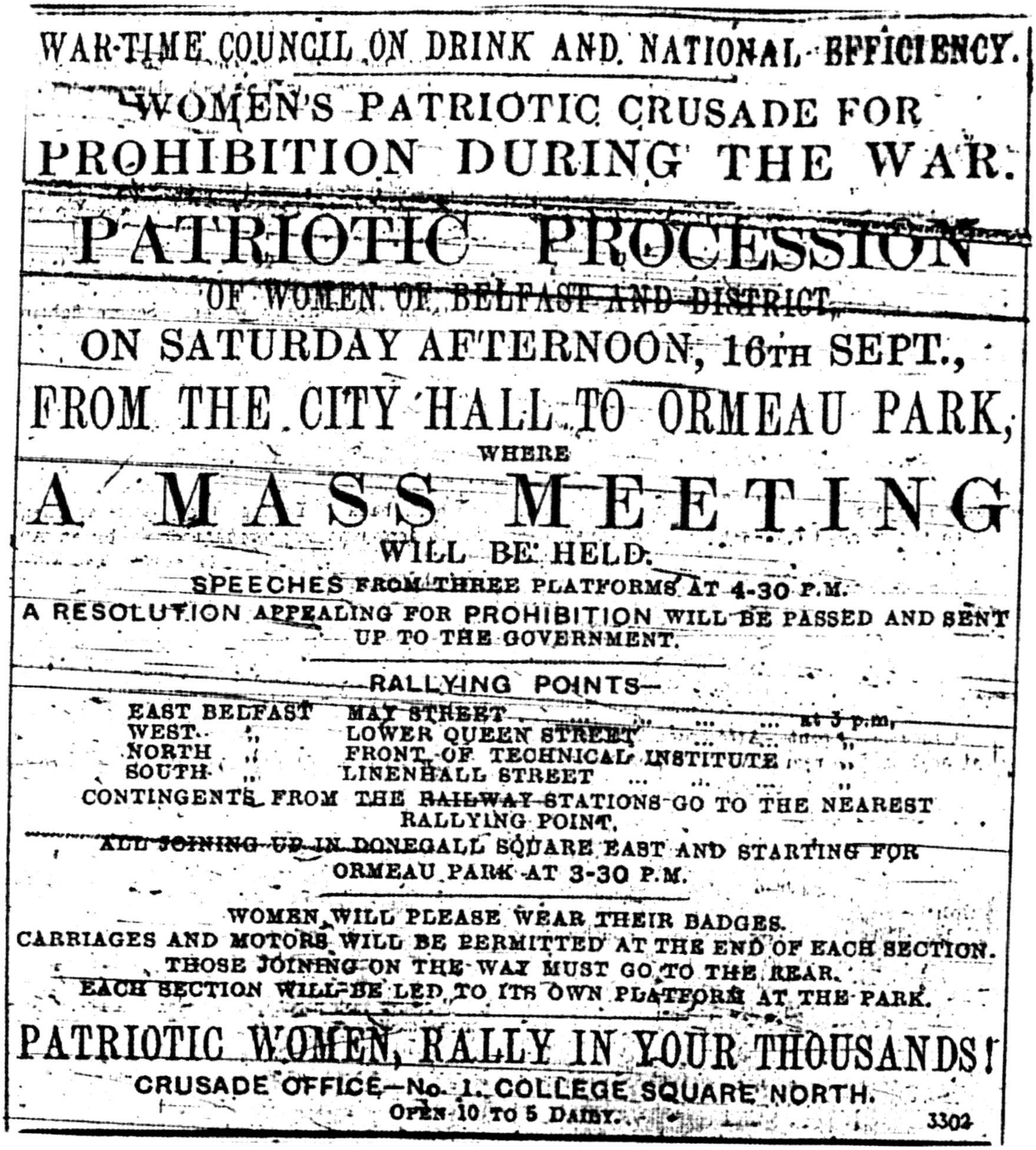

WAR-TIME COUNCIL ON DRINK AND NATIONAL EFFICIENCY.

WOMEN'S PATRIOTIC CRUSADE FOR PROHIBITION DURING THE WAR.

PATRIOTIC PROCESSION

OF WOMEN OF BELFAST AND DISTRICT,

ON SATURDAY AFTERNOON, 16TH SEPT.,

FROM THE CITY HALL TO ORMEAU PARK,

WHERE

A MASS MEETING

WILL BE HELD.

SPEECHES FROM THREE PLATFORMS AT 4-30 P.M.

A RESOLUTION APPEALING FOR PROHIBITION WILL BE PASSED AND SENT UP TO THE GOVERNMENT.

—RALLYING POINTS—

EAST BELFAST MAY STREET ... ... at 3 p.m.
WEST " LOWER QUEEN STREET ... ... "
NORTH " FRONT OF TECHNICAL INSTITUTE ... "
SOUTH " LINENHALL STREET ... ... "

CONTINGENTS FROM THE RAILWAY STATIONS GO TO THE NEAREST RALLYING POINT.

ALL JOINING UP IN DONEGALL SQUARE EAST AND STARTING FOR ORMEAU PARK AT 3-30 P.M.

WOMEN WILL PLEASE WEAR THEIR BADGES.
CARRIAGES AND MOTORS WILL BE PERMITTED AT THE END OF EACH SECTION.
THOSE JOINING ON THE WAY MUST GO TO THE REAR.
EACH SECTION WILL BE LED TO ITS OWN PLATFORM AT THE PARK.

PATRIOTIC WOMEN, RALLY IN YOUR THOUSANDS!

CRUSADE OFFICE—No. 1, COLLEGE SQUARE NORTH.
OPEN 10 TO 5 DAILY. 3302

6 September 1916

The war was evenly reported in all newpapers and patriotism during the war was encouraged in news reports as well as in advertising. New restrictions applied to the whole island in October 1918.

Drastic Lighting Restrictions.

FULL TEXT OF IRISH ORDER.

It is understood that the following lighting restrictions, as finally adopted by the Coal Controller's Department, have now been approved by the Lord Lieutenant. It is expected an official order will be issued at an early date.

1.—All shop window lighting and lighting outside shops and other premises is prohibited.

2.—Shops and warehouses, wholesale and retail, and offices connected therewith, save as hereinafter provided, shall be closed not later than 5-30 p.m. on Monday, Tuesday, Wednesday, and Thursday, not later than 7 p.m. on Friday, and not later than 9-30 p.m. on Saturday of each week.

A.—Chemists' shops may be opened at any hour for preparation of prescriptions or sale of medical requisites only; and dairies for the sale of milk only.

B.—Temperance refreshment establishments, and the establishments of hairdressers, tobacconists, and newsagents, may be kept open for the serving of customers to 9-30 p.m., but the quantity of gas or electricity used therein shall not exceed 50 per cent. of the quantity used in 1914.

3.—Licensed houses (i.e., licensed for consumption on the premises, and not including spirit groceries) must be closed between 3-30 and 6 p.m., and may be kept open between 6 p.m. and 9-30 p.m.

A.—Licensed hotels and restaurants may be opened for the service of meals, without intoxicating drink, between 3-30 and 6 p.m., but no meals shall be cooked therein after 8 p.m.

4.—The quantity of gas or electricity allowed to private houses, hotels, clubs, restaurants, boarding houses, and to offices not working in conjunction with shops, warehouses, and factories shall not be more than two-thirds the quantity consumed in 1914.

5.—Entertainments, meetings and other assemblies in theatres, public halls, and other places of amusement must terminate not later than 10-30 p.m.

Theatres, picture-houses and other places of entertainment open to the public during the daytime shall be closed on five days each week from 2-30 p.m. to 5-30 p.m., excepting by permit, which may be issued for special performances by the Coal Controller. Outdoor lighting of theatres is prohibited; and the total allowance of gas or electricity to theatres and other similar places must not exceed 75 per cent. of the 1914 supply.

Those in the House of Commons were outraged at suggestions of religious or political discrimination.

BELFAST PRISON INQUIRY.

MR. HEALY'S PROTEST.

OBJECTION TO COMMISSIONER.

CENSORED CORRESPONDENCE.

When the House of Commons went into Committee on the Special Commission (Belfast) Prison Bill yesterday, Mr. T. M. Healy moved the insertion of the name of the Lord Chief Justice of Ireland in place of that of the Right Hon. Wm. Huston Dodd as Chairman of the Commission. He did not want, he said, to cast any reflection on the name or impartiality of the learned judge mentioned in the bill. He made his motion solely on religious grounds, and his only reason for mentioning the Lord Chief Justice was in order to enable him to make his protest. The Government originally promised that the inquiry should be conducted by a Catholic official—namely, The MacDermot. Without any explanation, they proceeded to appoint a Presbyterian judge. He wanted to know the reason for the change, as he regarded it as a monstrous reflection cast upon a blameless official, a gentleman of ancient lineage, who had conducted himself in his official position without reproach. Some explanation was called for. He contended that the subject matter of the inquiry was one which affected the rights of the Catholic religion and Catholic bodies, and in such a matter a Catholic official should be the person to inquire into it. Some judge should be appointed who understood the nature of the indignities which were offered to these ninety unfortunate persons.

CHIEF SECRETARY'S REPLY.

Mr. Shortt said that he could not accept the amendment. The honourable gentleman had asked for an explanation of why, after having announced The MacDermot as the judge, the Government made an alteration. When last the question was raised in the House he (the Chief Secretary) discussed the question of the constitution of the tribunal with him as a private member of the House. Later he saw in the newspapers that the hon. and learned member was counsel for one of the parties whose case was to come before the tribunal. He (Mr. Shortt), therefore, ceased to discuss the matter with him, and he set up some other tribunal instead of The MacDermot. There was no question of politics or religion in the appointment of Mr. Justice Dodd. If the suggestions made in the affidavit were true, it wanted no Catholic to know that their treatment was outrageous. From the way the hon. member talked, one would think that the prisoners who made the charges were the persons who were being tried; but they were bringing charges against the prison officials, the doctor, and the police. Was it suggested that for that reason they were to choose the colour, religious and political, of the person who was to preside? That was a monstrous suggestion. There was nothing which could be suggested in any considerable way against Mr. Justice Dodd.

Mr. Healy said that the revelations which the Chief Secretary had made did not do him much credit. He asked at that table suggestions from him (Mr. Healy), and he suggested in the House the appointment of The MacDermot. He was never counsel for any of the prisoners, neither by brief nor retainer. The newspaper paragraph appeared months after he made the suggestion as to the appointment of the judge, and, because he suggested The MacDermot, the Chief Secretary now turned round. The right hon. gentleman had some reason to be ashamed of the transaction, because he censored his own letter to him (Mr. Healy). He sent his reply to the Chief Secretary to the Press.

As late as 30 December 1918 readers of the *Irish News* would have read of the 'Irish Belfastman' Joseph Devlin's election victory in West Belfast in which he resoundingly defeated Eamon de Valera of Sinn Fein. His victory speech gave no hint of bigotry and invited 'the Protestant toilers to join with us, their Catholic fellow-countrymen, in the great organised battle against reaction and Toryism in this city.'

Apart from the debate regarding the teaching of history, the seditious nature of which is not evident in a study of the textbooks used, most other matters relating to education appear to have been non-divisive before partition. Contemporary materials show that there were friendly relations between Protestant and Catholic teachers and people of both religions could support fundraising events for schools for only one. The same textbooks were used to educate all children at National schools, regardless of the religious affiliation of the school. The obligatory subjects, reading, handwriting, mathematics and geography, were taught in the same way in all schools.

Schools catered to the needs of the pupils in the surrounding areas and because of settlement patterns, especially in Belfast, this usually meant that the pupils were either Catholic or Protestant. There was nothing, however, to exclude a pupil from a school on the grounds of religion and some children did attend schools which did not teach their religion. The fact that religious emblems were not allowed in National schools would have made this less problematic. It must be remembered, however, that religion was taught in all schools and because of that all children did learn about one religion or another. That this would have occurred in churches anyway means that it was not schools per se which caused division.

The school-days' memories of Ena, Norman, Annie, Johnny, Mary, John and Teresa corroborate this view of education as found in source materials from 1910 to 1920. They recall being taught in the same manner, learning the same way and, with the exception of history, covering the same curriculum. They do not recall religion as being an important school subject nor as causing division in school. Far more important to them at the time were the daily copperplate handwriting lessons. All had the same respect for teachers, and homeworks were always done out of fear of repercussions the next day. That history was taught to Ena, Johnny and Teresa and not to Norman, Annie, Mary and John could indicate that there was some truth in newspaper claims about the teaching of history. However, it could equally indicate that teachers in mainly Protestant schools ignored the teaching of history because they were uncomfortable with the subject. Perhaps they preferred to exclude all history, rather than teach only British history and ignore Irish topics.

All those who were remembering their youth had extremely similar family and home backgrounds. Religion made no difference to family size which was larger than today. Teresa was one of eleven children while Annie had eight brothers and sisters. The majority of their fathers were born outside Belfast and all had a skilled trade or profession. Only two mothers worked and both did so because of necessity, Johnny's mother to support her family and Annie's to supplement the family budget. It is interesting that they earned this money with businesses within their homes and religion had no bearing on their need to work.

Everyone lived in a house which had no inside toilet, six in terrace houses and one in a cottage. Only one person, John, was in a house which was owned by his family and both Mary and Teresa were used to having no running water inside. In all homes there was a Christian ethos, Sunday attendance at Church, siblings, fathers in employment, sufficient plain food, warm clothes and shoes. Annie, Mary and Teresa portray slightly poorer versions in that Annie's mother had to occasionally pawn clothes, Mary's father had to travel to find work and Teresa's mother had to raise a large family alone after her husband died. Mary, Johnny and Teresa lived in towns outside Belfast for all or part of their youth, yet their home backgrounds are very similar to those who lived in the city. No aspect of their homes, employment, clothing, income or food could be said to be different because of their religion. They all learned and spoke the same language at home.

No one saw themselves, as children, as anything other than Irish and all played with children of other religions. None of them felt that there was anywhere that they could not go because of their religion. Norman's assertion that 'there was always the Falls and there was always the Shankill' may be coloured by his later experiences as a commercial traveller. Certainly no one remembers any bigoted comments in their homes and everyone points out that their parents also mixed with people of different religions. Ena's father went for a drink with Protestants, one was an Orangeman, and even employed a Protestant as a housekeeper when his wife died. Norman's parents had Catholic friends who were of such standing that they used the back door and John's mother was very friendly with her Catholic neighbours. Annie's father's shop catered to the whole community and Johnny's mother set up her business in a mainly Protestant town and stayed there all her life. Mary's parents had known of Catholics who looked after Protestant farms at the twelfth of July and Teresa smiled fondly when she recalled the Merlin brothers in their collarettes.

Activities after school were exactly the same for all seven. They did their homework and then played similar games with friends. Except for Mary everyone went to cinemas and her non-attendance had no religious connotations. Picture houses and music halls were frequented by patrons of all denominations. The fact that some churches introduced the cinematograph perhaps assisted in its elevation to respectability. Sports events too were attended by all and shopping on the Shankill had no religious undertones. The pragmatic Belfast people went where their money bought the most.

While Ena, Norman, Annie, Johnny, Mary, John and Teresa are of different religions, their memories of missions in their youth are very similar. There is no hint in their recollections that they viewed the missions they attended as especially Catholic or Protestant. Missions were another form of entertainment and an activity to take part in during leisure hours and, like the majority of recreational pursuits of the time, not always divided along religious lines.

No religious or cultural differences emerge from any of the memories of the shortage of money in their youth or the need to have food on the table. They spent any money they acquired in the same way and were under the same threat of sickness, especially tuberculosis. Holidays and travel were a luxury that few enjoyed.

The childhoods of Norman, Ena, Annie, Johnny, Mary, John and Teresa were, in the areas of home background, education and leisure activities, so alike that they could be described as having a common heritage. These seven people have a shared background which is indicative of the same ethnic identity. The fact that Johnny saw Edward Carson and John went to hear Eamon de Valera shows that even some political aspects were interchangeable. More importantly, when discussing each person's response with the other, it is clear that they view themselves as having had a common heritage in childhood. Each one, when hearing the other people's responses to the questions, said, 'Didn't I tell you we were all the same then?'

It is only when discussing the violence which took place at the end of the decade that they reveal the differing attitudes that entered their society. All feel that trust, which had been so much a part of their childhoods, ended and that the idea of the 'other side' began, not with partition, but with the violence which surrounded it.

Looking at the north-east of Ireland in the years 1910 to 1920 appears to reveal different and sometimes contradictory facets of a period in history. It was usual for Catholics and Protestants to interact with each other in all areas, workplace, home, shopping, leisure activities, and sectarianism was viewed as something to be scorned.

Entertainment was not divided along religious lines in advertising and attendance, or in the memory of those who were alive then. Sporting events were not divided in a sectarian manner and support of teams was little different than supporting Everton or Arsenal today. While education may have taken place in different buildings, it was very similar and rarely divisive.

According to some of the ordinary people who lived then, each viewing the period from a different religious perspective, attitudes changed because of the loss of trust which followed the violence surrounding partition. However, before that time, their memories emphasise a sense of common interests and identity as children and this is corroborated by the source material which relates to mundane, everyday life.

Perhaps this is why Lynn Doyle wrote with such optimism at the time:

> Who shall appraise the value of common aims, and common interests and common memories; of mutual knowledge, when we have discarded our blind guides, and know one another as we are, not as we are feigned to be? Who knows but my friend's little grandson and mine may some-day stand hand in hand with swelling bosoms when the drums break forth, and orange and green come down the road together in memory of dead Irishmen who fought in diverse causes, and sometimes with one another, but always for Ireland.
>
> (1921)

Bibliography

Akenson,D.H. 1973.The Control of Schooling in Northern Ireland. Belfast: Institute of Irish Studies.
Bardon,J. 1992.A History of Ulster . Belfast : Blackstaff Press.
Boal,F.W. 1987.Northern Ireland: Geographical Perspectives on an Ethnically Polarised Society', Canadian Journal of Irish Studies,XII (2): 33 - 42 .
Buckley,Anthony. 1989.'The Spirit of Irish Sectarianism',The Canadian Journal of Irish Studies,XV (2):23 - 29.
Coolahan,J. 1981 Irish Education- History and Structure, Dublin: Institute of Public Administration.
Crosbie,Jane E.M. 1990 A Tour of the Ardes,1910-35, Belfast: Friar's Bush Press.
Curtin,C., and T.M.Wilson 1989. Ireland From Below. Galway: Galway University Press.
Dowling,P.J. 1971.A History of Irish Education. Cork: Mercier Press.
Doyle,Lynn 1921. An Ulster Childhood. Maunsel & Roberts,reprinted Blackstaff Press,Belfast.
Evans,E.Estyn 1977. Ireland's Eye,The Photographs of Robert John Welch. Belfast,Blackstaff Press.
Foster,R.F. 1988. Modern Ireland. London: Penguin Books
--------------1989.Varieties of Irishness in M.Crozier(ed.) Cultural Traditions in Northern Ireland,Belfast: Institute of Irish Studies: 5 - 24.
Gallagher,E. 1989.At Points of Need - The Story of the Belfast Central Mission. Blackstaff Press.
Gray,J.1992. 'Popular Entertainment', in Beckett et al (eds), Belfast,The Making of the City, 1800 - 1914, Belfast: Appletree Press
Gribbon,Sybil 1982. Edwardian Belfast,A Social Profile. Appletree Press.
Harris,R. 1972. Prejudice and Tolerance in Ulster. Manchester: University Press.
Humphries,S. 1984. Recording Life Stories. Inter-Action trust.

Johnstone,H. 1987.'McQuiston Memorial Presbyterian Church', Journal

of the East Belfast Historical Society. 2(2) :32 - 35.(1987)
Kennedy,Billy,(Ed.) 1990.A Celebration:1690-1990,The Orange Institution, The Orange Institution.
Kennedy,Dennis 1987.The Widening Gulf. Belfast Blackstaff Press.(1987)
Maguire,W.A. 1986. Caught in Time -The Photographs of Alex Hogg. Belfast: Friar's Bush Press.
McKeever,G.(ed.) 'Great Matches of Belfast Celtic F.C.' in Up The Falls, Falls Community Council History Project, Part Two.
Open,M. 1985. Fading Lights,Silver Screens. Antrim: Greystone Books.
O Tuathaigh,G. 1988. 'From United Kingdom to Divided Island: Aspects of the Irish Experience 1850 - 1922. in Bartlett,Curtin,O'Dwyer.O Tuathaigh (eds.), Irish Studies, A General Introduction. Dublin:Gill and Macmillan: 126 - 151.
Stewart,A.T.Q. 1967.The Ulster Crisis. London: Faber and Faber.
----------------- 1977.The Narrow Ground. London: Faber and Faber.
Taylor,L.J. 1989. 'The Mission: An Anthropological View of an Irish Religious Occasion', in Curtin and Wilson, 1 - 22.
Thompson,P. 1988 The Voice of the Past. Oral History, Oxford: Oxford University Press.
Toelken,Barre 1979.The Dynamics of Folklore. Boston: Houghton Mifflin.(1979)
Tonkin,Elizabeth 1992 Narrating Our Pasts. Cambridge: Cambridge University Press.
Walker,B.M. & Dixon,H. 1983 No Mean City, Belfast 1880 - 1914. Friar's Bush Press.
Wilson,William A. 1979. 'Folklore & History: Fact Amid the Legends', in J.H.Brunvand (ed.), Readings in American Folklore. New York: W.W.Norton & Company:449 - 67.

Note: Sadly Johnny Marquis, Teresa McCallam and Mary Thompson have died since I began researching this work. Ena (almost ninety-five), Norman (ninety), Annie (ninety-six), and John (almost ninety-three) are all still living in their own homes.

Allison Murphy, December 1999